The Neighborhood

Jennifer Lee Bannwolf

Copyright © 2022

All Rights Reserved

ISBN: 978-1-954850-86-6

Dedication

For my two Angels.

To my family and friends who love me no matter what.

For my husband, who believes in me and our dreams!

I would be lost without you!

Love you all to the moon and back!

To pieces and so, so much more!

Acknowledgment

First and foremost, I have to thank my amazing husband, Brad, for Michael's inspiration and for always supporting me!

You have been my rock!

You've always believed in me no matter what job I had or whatever I worked on. I can't thank you enough, and I am so glad we get to share our lives together!

To my sister, Rachel, who is the strongest woman and mother I know to the two most beautiful girls in the world!! You inspire me every day to be strong and keep going! You were always the best big sister - love you to pieces!

To Emily, my writer sister, love you so much. Thanks for inspiring me!

To my best friend Sarah, aka my Saleen. You have always been an inspiration to me with your career as an X-ray technician and now doing the mammogram.

I'm so happy your stars aligned, and you and Travis and the boys found each other!! You have been a rock-solid friend who supports me through all and her mother, Sherri, who pushed me to follow my dreams!!

You are both such strong inspirational women who I admire!

To Sandy, an amazing friend, and Val, for two readings that were life-changing!

To Nancy, who, with the utmost care, let me have a few days off after our baby Harley passed. They aren't just animals. They are family!

To my teachers, Earl, Holly, Gail, Jean, Coralee, and Deb, you all are so amazing, and I can never thank you enough for leading me to my career that I love so much!

To Judy and Stephanie, friends who are badass businesswomen who inspire me every day!! Shout out to All About the Gown by Judy in Lake Geneva, Wi!! If you're getting married, go there, period!!

To my mom and dad, who taught me just to be a good human and hard worker!

To my husband's side of the family, who is always there for us day or night! I'm so lucky to be a part of such an amazing family!

To all the friends and family along my path who have listened to my craziness and all my stories for years, thank you from the bottom of my heart for being there for me!!

Kindness is infectious, and we need more of it in this world!

Love you all!

Keep dreaming because life gets better when you believe!

CONTENTS

Dedication iii

Acknowledgment iv

About the Author ix

Preface xi

Chapter 1: Eve 1

Chapter 2: Sammy 13

Chapter 3: The Neighborhood 26

Chapter 4: Growing Up 39

Chapter 5: Devices and Vices 52

Chapter 6: Fight or Flight 63

Chapter 7: School Days 75

Chapter 8: Troys' Oyster Bar 84

Chapter 9: The Hospital 94

Chapter 10: The Party 106

Chapter 11: He Asked Me Out 119

Chapter 12: The Angel Kids 129

Chapter 13: School Party 139

Chapter 14: Home Sweet Home 154

Chapter 15: Finding Out 166

Chapter 16: Confronting Cameron 177

Chapter 17: The Festival 188

Chapter 18: The Big Secret 198

Chapter 19: Vulnerability 209

Chapter 20: Planning Trips and Dreams 222

Epilogue 233

About the Author

Jennifer resides in Illinois with her husband and two pug/chihuahua puppies.

She is a licensed massage therapist who loves her career. Her passion is writing, reading, cooking, singing, and crafting. She lives for being around her family and friends. She believes that each day is a gift and that life should be lived to its fullest.

Preface

Loss.

We all inevitably have to face it at some point in our lives. It's because we're human, and we only have a certain number of years to live and learn. I myself have had so much loss in my life that writing this book just came naturally to me. It's something that changes us forever for better or worse, but we are changed, without a doubt.

In the past few years, we have also experienced loss and mourning for our freedoms. Something as normal as the sun rising to us a few years ago is now looked at with much more appreciation and love. Writing is a gift. I have written many things in my life but have never dared to have them published.

To be published, to be read by so many people, to reveal a part of me that has been so buried deep for so long is terrifying. Yes, this is fiction, but bits and pieces are from my life experience and losses.

This book is for laughter, healing, and love.

This book is for all the mothers and fathers who have lost a child.

This book is for all the people who enjoy a little supernatural twist.

I mean, who wouldn't fall in love with a woman who is a little crazy, drinks too much, and goes to very expensive therapy sessions, all while living a life of luxury with her entrepreneurial husband and two lovable dogs.

Yes, I promise you this book is funny, loving, and will touch your heart! And hey, just a bonus: you may get some end of the world survival tips.

Chapter 1

Eve

Evelyn Moskowitz stood at the balcony, soaking up the last rays of the setting sun. Her russet hair was undone, falling down her shoulders in golden-brown waves. She had her eyes closed, and her petite frame seemed relaxed, almost completely at ease.

This was how Michael Moskowitz found his wife when he entered the living room that was connected to their balcony. He paused for a moment, admiring the way her long lashes brushed against her high cheekbones and the halo the sun's rays made around her glossy hair. He thought she looked like an angel.

Evelyn, as if she had heard him, turned back to look at him with slight surprise.

"I thought you had to stay back late?" she said.

Michael shook his head slightly and said, "I did, but the boys got done with the land scraping early, and I didn't have the heart to make them start hauling in the cement. Plus…" Michael moved toward Evelyn and wrapped an arm around her shoulders. "I kind of wanted to spend our last days in this house together."

Eve turned to look at Michael, admiring the way his short brown hair was mussed up in a way that belied his age – he looked almost boyish.

"That's extremely thoughtful of you," she said, then narrowed her eyes. "Are you sure it's not because I told you we could order in and have sushi today?"

Michael grinned, his blue eyes lighting up with mirth. He moved his arm away from Evelyn's shoulder and held a hand to his chest, pouting in mock hurt.

"I would never!" he said with a dramatic gasp, mimicking a character from the Gossip Girl series that Evelyn had made him watch with her.

Evelyn rested both hands on her waist and looked up at Michael with an exacting gaze. Michael grinned. He had almost forgotten how cute she was when she did that. She was short, way shorter than most women, but the way she glared up at him was always so intimidating. He held his hands up as if caught.

"Okay, okay, you caught me." He winked at her and watched as her fake glare broke out into a beautiful smile.

"Ugh, I hate sushi," she groaned as she wrinkled her nose.

"I know," Michael replied with a cheeky grin, already starting to order.

THE NEIGHBORHOOD

Evelyn scowled. Her husband could be very childish sometimes. But then he also made her laugh.

"I'm gonna go get some of those bread rolls you like," Michael informed her after he had put down the phone.

Evelyn brightened up, her emerald eyes shining with glee.

"Yes! Thank you. Thank you. Thank you!" she said, positively beaming.

That was the thing about them. They always got along very well together. Michael loved sushi, and she disliked it. She loved bread rolls, and Michael thought they were bland. So, they usually took turns deciding on what they were going to eat. That day just so happened to be Michael's turn, hence the sushi. The bread roll place did not do deliveries, but he always made sure that she also got to eat her favorite foods. He had always been thoughtful.

Evelyn twisted the necklace she was wearing around her neck absentmindedly as she set up the movie they were going to watch, *"Ten Things I Hate About You."*

It was probably Michael's favorite rom-com. He pretended he hated all the stuff she made him watch but really, he watched them with more attention than she ever did. She had almost caught him shedding a tear when they had watched *'The Fault in Our Stars'* for the first time.

She looked around at the living room, thinking of the memories they had made there. The doorbell rang. It was Michael. They worked quietly as they set up the table together. Then they sat on the couch while they ate, the movie playing in front of them.

But nobody was looking at the movie. Michael, who usually commented on the many reasons to like Heath Ledger, was silent, for once.

Evelyn figured the packaged boxes of belongings had prompted his somber mood because he was usually never quiet. She pulled his hand in hers, but he pulled them away instead of turning to her, trying to smile.

"You're shutting down your clinic?" he asked.

Evelyn was a chiropractor, and she had her own practice. She had been so proud of the Doctorate of Chiropractic Certificates that hung on the wall, but then she had to take them down and pack them away into boxes with the rest of their stuff.

"I'm not," she told him.

Michael knew she was lying. "Don't, Evelyn. We're just shifting it."

"I don't want to work anymore," Evelyn told him, averting her gaze.

This time he knew she was telling him the truth.

THE NEIGHBORHOOD

"Why?" he asked.

"We already earn enough with the restaurant, and I want to take a break for a bit."

"Oh," Michael said. "I thought you were giving up on your practice."

"No. Why would I give it up?" Evelyn told him, half laughing. "I have this amazing skill; I'm going to use it."

To anyone else, it would seem Evelyn was talking about her chiropractor practice, but Michael knew she was talking about her clairaudience. Ever since she had been young, Evelyn had been an 'empath.' She had a painfully accurate intuition, and she had this gift that enabled her to listen to people's conscience and somehow sense their aura. Unfortunately, she was also afflicted with visitation dreams at times.

Michael smiled at her. They finished eating. Then Michael poured them both a glass of wine, twinned Evelyn's hand with his, and took them around for one last tour of the house with all their belongings in it. They were still going to be staying there for a few more days, but it would not be quite the same living in an almost entirely empty house. The hall was filled with boxes, but their furniture had already been packed and sent to the next house they had bought. Finally, it was empty, and their footsteps echoed slightly. Michael took her to their bedroom first.

"This. This is where we came up with the plan for Angel's Light."

Evelyn laughed. She remembered it so clearly. She had been reading a book, and Michael had been scrolling aimlessly on his phone when all of a sudden, he had sat up and announced.

"Let's start a restaurant."

She had asked him what had inspired him to start a restaurant when he could barely cook, and he had just shrugged and told her that his mother had been a bad cook too, and it was not his fault he had been passed down those genes. She laughed, but she had taken him seriously because despite his playfulness, Michael had an eye for detail and the brains to start and keep up a business. So they had sat for fifteen hours straight, only stopping for snack breaks, and brainstormed their new restaurant plan.

"I thought you had lost it when you told me that," she informed him.

Michael half-smirked at the memory.

"I *was* sort of impulsive," he admitted. "But it all worked out in the end, didn't it?"

Evelyn almost scowled, but he was right. It *had* worked out alright in the end. Between Michael's construction business and her chiropractic practice, they had had enough funds to start the restaurant and build it from the ground up. They had called it 'Angel's Light,' simply because Evelyn had found the name catchy at the time. It consisted of one floor, a retired Michelin star chef whose only job was to overlook and guide the newer chefs and entire waiting staff.

It had started off to become really popular, partly because of the name and partly because Evelyn and Michael were somewhat famous as a 'power couple' amongst their friends, so they had been inclined to try. It was also successful because of the wide variety of cuisines.

Michael and Evelyn had made sure to add both sushi and bread rolls to the menu list, along with three kinds of pasta, Chinese food, and later, a cocktail bar. After its initial popularity had waned, it remained a favorite of the locals and generated more income than they expected in profit. In one line in the Times, it had also been mentioned as a very 'hip, and upcoming' restaurant, so new clientele occasionally came to try it out.

Evelyn pulled them away from the bedroom toward the kitchen. "Remember the first time you cooked here?"

Michael sighed heavily, shaking his head in mock dismay. "How could I ever forget!?" he said.

"Even if you tried to, I wouldn't let you forget," Evelyn said, smirking up at him.

"You're evil," Michael told her, suppressing a smile.

Evelyn laughed. She imagined the scene as it had happened. It had been their one-year anniversary, and Michael had tied to bake a cake while she made their anniversary dinner. Then, the doorbell had rung, and Evelyn had gone to check on whoever was at the door.

Michael had taken it upon himself to 'flambe' the rosette pasta, pouring some alcohol over the flame and brandishing the pan just like, as he had later explained how they 'did in the movies.' Evelyn had come back to the kitchen to find her pasta ruined, swimming in alcohol. While she and Michael desperately tried to salvage it, they had broken out into an argument, forgetting all about the cake.

The cake had burnt to a crisp and started to smoke, but neither of them realized it till the fire alarm started ringing. Evelyn had not even known burnt cake could emit so much smoke. Suffice it to say, Michael had slept on the couch that night, and they had both not had any food that day.

It had seemed like the world's worst first anniversary back then, but the memory of it made the pair laugh in the later years to come. Michael had vehemently tried and succeeded at improving at cooking, going as far as to take cooking classes. He no longer tried to 'flambe' like the movies showed and were slightly less chaotic in the kitchen.

Michael dragged them toward the bathroom.

"Remember the first time we showered together?" he asked with a glint in his eye. "You had this-"

Evelyn slapped a hand to his mouth, cutting him off and muffling the rest of his words beneath her palm. Michael made a sound of protest deep in his throat and then licked her hand.

Evelyn balked, pulling her hand away in extreme disgust as Michael broke off into raucous laughter.

"You are a *child*. An *absolute child*!" she exclaimed, wiping her hand on his shirt. She scowled, watching him laugh. Finally, she dragged him, still laughing, to the living room, where he took one look at her revolted expression and broke into a fresh bout of laughter. Evelyn tried but was unable to hold back the smile that pulled on her lips.

"What am I going to do with you?" she sighed, with a fond shake of her head.

"Love me?" Michael suggested.

Evelyn rolled her eyes. It was so like Michael to try and flirt his way out of everything he did.

"Too bad I already do."

'Too bad," Michael muttered, absently sitting on the couch and pulling her onto his lap. "Do you remember the first time we met?"

"The first time we met?" Evelyn hummed, then paused to think a bit. "No, I don't think so. You weren't really the memorable kind back then," she lied.

Michael scowled. "I was perfectly memorable."

"Were you?" Evelyn asked back, teasingly.

"Mhmm," Michael hummed. "You could not take your eyes off of me."

Evelyn grinned because she knew he was right. They had met at a bar in Iowa back when they were in college. Then, Evelyn had been fresh-faced and new to college life. Her friends had taken her to a salon that day and given her a drastic makeover. They had had her long hair cut into a boy cut forced, her into a pair of tottering heels, and a cute white dress that complimented the melted chocolate hue of her hair and the spring green of her eyes.

Then they had given her the boldest makeup look and taken her out to the bar. She had seen Michael across the bar. He stood there with his friends. His brown hair was dyed black back then. He had the sharpest jawline she had seen on any man, and he was tall, taller than most boys she had met. Michael had felt her eyes on him, turned to look, and then smirked at her. He did not approach her, though. She had approached him.

She remembered the way his blue eyes widened in surprise when she asked him if she could buy him a drink. They had clicked instantly, somehow managing to find topics to talk about constantly for hours. She had asked him his name as she was about to leave.

"Thomas," he had told her, but she instantly realized he was lying. She let it slip, of course, because it was only reasonable that he gave her a fake name because of 'stranger danger.' So, she had told him he could call her 'Ivy.'

He knew she was lying too.

They thought they would never meet again. But they were both surprised when, just a week later, they caught each other's eyes across the college campus. He had been surrounded by his jock friends, and she had been hurrying to her classes.

They stopped to talk to each other, missing the tardy bell and skipping out on their classes. They clicked again, as easily as they had that night at the bar. They had given each other their real names then, and the rest was history.

Evelyn lifted her head off of Michael's shoulder.

"You know, I think I liked calling you Thomas more.

Maybe you should officially change your name," she told him.

Michael mock glared at her. "Anything for you, Ivy," he retorted.

Evelyn rolled her eyes. "Why did I marry you again?" she asked him.

"Because you love me," Michael told her.

"No. that's not it," Evelyn said. "It was definitely because you were a popular jock."

"Are you saying you married me for my reputation?" Michael asked her.

Evelyn grinned and said, "That's exactly what I'm saying. I'm glad you caught on."

Michael fondly shook his head, and they sat in comfortable silence for a while, surrounded by taped-up boxes of belongings and old memories, each of them lost in their own thoughts. They both wondered, with trepidation, what the future held for them.

Chapter 2

Sammy

When morning came, Michael woke Evelyn up. They had spent the night on a mattress on the floor of the room, their bed frame having already been sent on ahead to their new place. They had dressed, shivering slightly in the chill in the air, packed their leftover belongings, and driven to meet the realtor who was supposed to meet them at their new residence. Evelyn had had a late night.

She had not been able to sleep till it was nearly midnight. Part of her had been hesitant about facing the nightmares that haunted her every night. But, eventually, she steeled herself, knowing that the next day, she had to be at the top of her game. Handling the Palmer students starting their internship with her in the morning would be challenging.

They waited for the realtor outside their apartment, yawning and occasionally checking the time on their wristwatches. Then, finally, Michael asked, "Ready to go?"

Evelyn nodded in agreement, and they proceeded to bundle

up in their car. Michael drove while Evelyn sat beside him, cradling a cup of much-needed coffee.

"I think we might be slightly late," Michael said, pressing his foot on the breaks as they encountered the downtown rush hour traffic.

"Call her, maybe?" Evelyn suggested.

Michael nodded. He pulled out his phone to call. It rang once, then twice, and then it was picked up. Michael put his phone on speaker mode so that Evelyn could listen in.

"Hey, you guys!" A cheery voice called out from the phone speaker. "I was just beginning to wonder where you were."

Michael grinned at Evelyn, and she grinned back. They both realized there was something about their realtor's chirpy voice that they both liked. So maybe this would be it. The final house that they would decide on.

"Hey, Sammy," Evelyn said. "We're just wrestling with traffic right now. We should be there in 20 minutes if our GPS is correct."

"Sure," Samantha, the realtor, hummed from the phone. "Take all the time you need."

Twenty minutes later, they were pulling into the apartment complex. Michael called Samantha's phone, but the call rang twice, and then it was dropped.

Evelyn looked around the parking lot with mild curiosity.

"Where is she?" she asked, pushing her unbound hair into a ponytail, tying it up using the elastic on her wrist. Michael grinned and was about to say something along the lines of, "Don't know. I'm too busy admiring you right now."

But just as he opened his mouth to say those words, a clear voice rang out that answered Evelyn's question.

"Behind you, actually," the voice said. It was as clear as the ringing of bells on a summer breeze.

They both turned as if in sync. Evelyn's scarf fluttered slightly, and she wrapped it around herself tighter. Before them stood an extremely beautiful blonde woman. She held out the hand with the phone in it and smiled at them slightly sheepishly.

"I'm sorry for not picking up the call," she explained. "I figured you were calling to ask where I was, and I was already walking around the lot toward you, so I didn't bother. Guess I was right, huh?"

Evelyn opened her mouth as if to say something and then closed it back. She had never heard such an unusual reason for someone choosing not to pick up a call. What they didn't know was that this should have been the first hint that nothing about that particular neighborhood was normal.

"That's perfectly fine," Michael told the blonde woman, still looking slightly impatient. Evelyn knew he wanted to get back to work. His construction manager had been trying to get to him all day. Apparently, there was an emergency at work due to a mishap by one of the new workers, something about having heard the architect's blueprints wrong.

The blonde smiled, and as if by magic, both Michael and Evelyn forgot about what they had been impatient about. She had a stunning smile that lit up the room.

"Hi, I'm Samantha Rodriguez," she introduced herself to them. "But you can call me Sammy. We talked on the phone a while ago…"

Then she looked at Michael expectantly as he had been the one who had called her in the car. Michael nodded.

"Hey, Samantha - Sammy," he corrected himself mid-statement. "Yes, you were supposed to show me around and give me the keys."

"Correct," Samantha said brightly. She pulled out a key from a hidden pocket in her professional black skirt. She put the key in Michael's hand as he extended before her. Then to his surprise, she rummaged in her purse, pulled out a piece of paper, and gave it to him too.

"This is the blueprint of the building," she informed them. "Now, if you could please follow me, I will introduce you to the landlord."

Samantha turned on her dark, high heels and started to power walk away from them, her earrings dangled slightly, emphasizing the long curve of her neck and her elegant updo. Evelyn was somewhat impressed. She herself was a professional woman, but Sammy exuded a sort of elegance and charm that she felt she did not have. She started following Samantha, and Michael fell into step beside her.

"She's really impressive. I knew she would be a good investment when we hired her."

"Mhm," she agreed.

"Maybe we can get her to find another location for the restaurant. I was thinking that we could open up another branch," Michael suggested, his voice lowered to a slight whisper.

"She's pretty too," Evelyn added, her eyes following the twenty-something-year-old realtor who walked before them. "She has the most gorgeous blue eyes."

Michael hummed thoughtfully at that. "Yeah, she is, though I do think green eyes are the prettiest."

With that, Michael winked at Evelyn, who had been looking at him with surprise. Evelyn was not the type to blush easily, but she blushed now. The red flush in her cheeks only brought out the green in her eyes.

"Shush, stop flirting with me here," she whispered back harshly.

Michael grinned contentedly in response but said nothing more.

"Aren't realtors supposed to look like older, Stepford wives? Huh, I guess there is a reason she's known as the neighborhood angel who brings people to this area," Evelyn said to herself.

Michael overheard her. His forehead creased slightly as his thoughts wandered from Samantha to Dale, the landlord they were about to be introduced to.

"I hope we find Dale as agreeable as we find Sammy," he muttered absentmindedly in response to Evelyn.

Evelyn paused for a moment to admire how handsome he looked when he creased his brow in a particular way. Then said, out loud.

"Well, we need a home, not some rental with a slumlord named Dale, who hits on me every second of his drunken day."

THE NEIGHBORHOOD

Michael snorted as he laughed. He pushed a fist to his mouth, disguising his chuckle as a cough. He looked at Evelyn, his eyes glinting with mirth. Samantha, too, giggled slightly.

"I assure you, he's no slumlord," she told them. "But, Dale is sort of an alcoholic. However, he is very friendly."

Samantha stopped in front of a huge mansion with an outer metal gate that said 4144.

"Here you are!" she told them, catching Evelyn's eye and smiling slightly to reassure her. The house was definitely not one that a slum lord would have possessed. It was beautiful. It was huge and had vast, luscious gardening spaces. It was just what Evelyn had had in mind.

'This is it,' Evelyn mouthed to Michael, her eyes glinting in excitement. She had landed her dream job in Maine, and she had finally found her dream house too. The excitement was building inside her. She could hardly wait to examine everything. She noticed a company car outside the house but was too busy exploring the perfectly manicured lawn. Samantha watched their joy with a collected smile. She waited till they finished looking around the house. Then she ushered them into the car.

"I'm hoping to show you around and point out a few things. Is that okay?" Samantha asked patiently, waiting for Evelyn to nod in agreement before she started the car. Once she had her approval, she started the car.

The engine purred to life immediately, and Samantha nosed the car toward the gate with practiced ease.

"Look," Samantha pointed at a man standing near the end of the lane. He was built like a beast and carried a gun. He nodded to Samantha when he saw her. "We have security guards assigned, twenty-four hours a day, for every street. That's Ruger. He's yours."

Evelyn and Michael leaned closer to the window as they drove past Ruger to get a good look at him and try and memorize his face. The man saluted smartly as the car passed them. His uniform was stretched taut by the bulky muscles hidden underneath them.

"Ruger seems hot," Evelyn joked.

Samantha faltered slightly on the wheel, and Michael coughed in surprise, but he had expected her to say something like that. Michael looked at her with exaggerated annoyance, but she grinned back at him. He had come to realize that his wife was a jokester. She had the sense of humor of a twenty-year-old.

"Babe, don't scare Sammy. She's driving," Michael told Evelyn.

Evelyn rolled her eyes playfully, huffing a little. Samantha regained her professionalism.

"If you prefer a female, we can arrange it," she informed Michael, and Evelyn couldn't help laughing at that. Michael tried to hide his grin as he realized that Samantha was sincere about her offer.

Evelyn grinned and said, "No. Ruger sounds just fine. Thank you."

Michael looked at her in mock warning before Samantha started to speak again.

"As I was saying, you have a personal car service at your disposal any time of the day or night. In addition, we have an emergency evacuation protocol class you will both need to attend and a firearms training course. Have you both been to a range before?" Samantha asked with a twinkle in her eye.

Evelyn caught Samantha's eye across the rearview mirror and nodded enthusiastically.

"Yes, we have," she said, grinning a little.

She looked at Michael to see that he was already looking at her with a grin of his own. She knew they were both reminiscing about the memories that they had made in the numerous shooting ranges they had visited together over the years. Evelyn remembered how, when they had first started dating, Michael, her jock boyfriend, had taken her to a range. She had been hesitant but also excited to learn something new.

She remembered the way she had taken one look at the guns and balked. She was a cheerleader. She was not used to extreme sports or guns. Michael had later teased her about her pale face and her fear of guns.

"Do you remember the time I took you to the range?" Michael asked Evelyn, proving that they had both been thinking the same thing.

"Extremely clearly," Evelyn said with a smile. She saw the entire scene play out in her mind's eye.

***

Michael pulled her frozen figure over to the guns, and she let him. She trusted Michael completely at this point. He picked up a black gun and tested its weight, then another and another, until he tested almost all the guns. Finally, he reached the last gun and then nodded slightly to himself. "This would be a perfect fit."

He dropped the gun softly into Evelyn's hands, muttering a quick thankful prayer that nobody else was using the range at that moment. Evelyn had recovered slightly enough to recognize the weight of the weapon in her hands. She turned it over, fear fading to curiosity.

"Shoot at the dummy," Michael told her. So she shot,

missing the dummy by a clean mile. Michael laughed slightly.

"No, you're not holding it correctly. See," he said.

Evelyn expected him to take the gun from her, but instead, Michael put his own hands over hers and guided her fingers with his own. He tightened his grip on the trigger but did not push it.

He brushed a few strands of her hair away from her face before wrapping his other hand around the gun.

"Take a deep breath," he told her.

Evelyn inhaled evenly.

"Now hold it, focus on the target," he continued whispering in her ear, making her heart flutter slightly. Finally, he led her hand high, aimed at the target, and held it there.

"Now shoot," he said, pressing the trigger beneath her finger with his own.

The bullet left the gun and flew through the air toward the dummy, hitting it right in the chest. Evelyn looked at the hold in the dummy, then at the gun, and then at the dummy again. Then she let out the loudest whoop of victory Michael had ever heard in his life.

"That was amazing!" she exclaimed, breathless with excitement. She leaped out of Michael's arms and toward the guns.

Then she weighed all of them on her own. She found a grey one that she thought fitted perfectly inside her palm as if it was made for her. She aimed at another dummy, then shot. It hit the dummy right in the head. Michael's jaw dropped.

"How?" he muttered. But Evelyn was too busy to notice. She shot the next target and then another one. She managed to shoot one of them in the throat and another in the chest.

"Woah, okay. Leave some of my fragile masculinity to myself, please," Michael joked.

Evelyn laughed. But that had been the start of her expertise at guns.

***

"I don't think I'm ever going to forget how good I am at range shooting and how atrocious you are at it," Evelyn said, pulling herself away from her memories and back into the present. She was only half-joking. Michael was by no means 'bad' at it, but Evelyn was incredibly talented when it came to guns.

Michael scowled, but he was mostly joking.

Samantha laughed at Evelyn's comment.

"Well, then, I'm sure you guys won't need practice classes. Perhaps a recreational trip then?" she spoke softly.

THE NEIGHBORHOOD

"That would be amazing. Thank you," Evelyn told her.

"Anyways, we just take precautions here at the neighborhood to make you all as safe as possible. Of course, there will be checkpoints we will go over as well," Samantha said. Michael and Evelyn nodded at the information, storing it into their heads for later use.

"Ah yes, one last thing," Samantha suddenly added, just as they all pulled into the driveway of 4144, and Evelyn and Michael were about to exit their car.

"Do you like kids?" she asked. "Because your neighbors to the left have two older ones. Good kids, you'll like them."

Evelyn felt her heart sink as memories came flooding in again, this time about her past. Michael noticed and wrapped an arm around his wife in a subtle attempt to comfort her. Evelyn managed to let her lips curl up into a smile, blocking out the memories of her past and the children she would have had.

"Yes, we love kids," she told Samantha, and her voice held a certain painful depth that resonated in the air long after they both had retired into their new home.

Chapter 3

The Neighborhood

Evelyn soaked up the perfect Maine sunlight. She was standing in the yard of her new house, waiting for Sammy to come and give her the keys to it so that they could officially move in. Eventually getting tired of standing still, she started walking. The beautiful yellow sundress that she had chosen to wear fluttered around her.

"This place is gorgeous!" Evelyn muttered under her breath. It was true. The whole subdivision seemed exactly like it was out of a movie set or a picture book. Every house had a perfectly kept yard. Some yards had creeper trellis growing along picket fences. Others had huge towering trees that provided a welcome shade against the sun's glare, and others, yet, had groomed garden yards that looked as breathtaking as a florist's shop. It made Evelyn wonder what she wanted to do with her yard.

"Should I turn it into a vegetable garden?" Evelyn mused and then shook her head. "No. I like the flowers and the trellis more. Maybe I'll plant some lavenders to make the house smell lovely."

THE NEIGHBORHOOD

She nodded to herself, satisfied with her train of thought.

Michael and Evelyn knew they had been lucky to find the perfect house in the seemingly perfect subdivision. They were luckier still because the house was only a twenty-minute drive away from Portland, which was where Evelyn's new chiropractic job was, yet it was still far away from the hustle and bustle of traffic. Thus, it was the perfect location for them to relax while keeping up with their jobs.

Evelyn cast a disdainful look at the delicate watch that glittered on her wrist. She subconsciously turned her lips into a pout as she wondered where Michael was. She was supposed to meet him at their house after he was finished with his work so that Samantha could hand us over the documents to sign over the deed of the house.

"Please don't be late," Evelyn whispered as if she could say those words to Michael herself. Then, as if summoned by those very words, a huge truck pulled up into the circular driveway. Evelyn watched as an equally built beast of a man got out of the truck and snorted slightly.

'Big truck for a big man,' she thought to herself, noting how cute Michael looked, despite coming straight from work.

She loved being a female, but she did think it was a lot of work. She sighed, thinking something along the lines of, 'If only I could look that good all the time.'

Michael grinned as he looked at his wife. He did not think Evelyn knew how pretty she looked in the sundress she was wearing. He loved the months when he got to see her all dressed up in her favorite summery outfits.

"Hi, Eve!" he called out cheerily. He walked past her to get to the door and smacked her butt as he did so. Evelyn shot him a side-eyed glare so piercing it would have made most people flinch, but Michael just grinned at her, cheekily sticking out his tongue briefly before shooting her a wink. He knew he would be in trouble when they got home. For some reason, Evelyn was shy about public affection, which was weird because she had once worked at a club off Sunset Avenue when she was still in her early twenties.

Michael noticed Samantha walking toward them and pointed her out to Evelyn.

They watched as the blonde girl walked up to them. She was dressed in her usual professional attire, and her heels clicked loudly against the pavement. Her blouse was a light peach-pink shade this time, and her skirt was white, adorned with a little bit of glitter but somehow still looked very professional on her.

"Good morning, Mr and Mrs Moskowitz," Samantha greeted them.

Evelyn coughed in slight surprise at being addressed so formally. She smiled warmly at the younger woman and said, "Please, Sammy, just call us Mike and Eve."

"Mike and Eve it is then,' Samantha said and then broke into a smile. "You look stunning, Mrs Mosko- oh sorry, *Eve.*"

Evelyn laughed slightly, a blush coming onto her cheeks.

"Thank you, sweetheart!" she told Samantha. Evelyn had felt slightly underdressed, but Michael's appraising gaze and Samantha's compliment had reassured her and put her into a surprisingly cheerful mood.

"Well, shall we get a look in the inside of the house then, Mike and Eve?" Samantha said, walking toward the door and unlocking it with the keys. She held open the door for them and entered only when they were safely inside.

"I think you'll love Bliss," Samantha said absentmindedly as she turned on the lights around the house.

"Bliss?" Michael asked.

"Oh," Samantha said, slightly embarrassed. "I forgot to tell you, but every house in this subdivision has a name."

"That's such a cute idea!" Evelyn cooed.

Samantha laughed slightly at that.

"Thank you, Eve. Please come this way," she said, leading them to the kitchen.

The kitchen was perfect. In fact, the entire house was perfect, almost too perfect. Every single detail, down to the backsplash in the kitchen, looked like something Michael and Eve would have picked themselves. It was precisely decorated and maintained as if to perfectly tailored to their tastes.

It had been constructed partly like a ranch and partly like a mansion. There were four bedrooms, fully furnished, with warm cherry wood floors and classic faux fur rugs to keep them warm in winters. All the bedrooms each had an en-suite walk-in closet and their own bathroom. The master bedroom was the largest.

Evelyn peered into the en-suite and squealed. "Oh my god. Michael, look!" she exclaimed. She pointed at the rain shower connected to a fireplace that looked inward into a hot tub bath that was large enough to fit two people.

Evelyn jumped into the bathtub, enraptured, suddenly youthful again.

"Oh, to come home after a taxing day at work and soak in a warm bubble bath with a glass of wine and a book," she recited dramatically, with a deep, wistful sigh at the end.

Both Michael and Samantha laughed at her enthusiasm.

Michael pulled her to himself and held her close.

"Aren't you just the cutest?" he asked, playfully pretending to pinch her cheeks.

Evelyn fake scowled up at him. "That's not what you thought back in high school," she said, wriggling out of his grip.

'Didn't I?" Michael mused, a twinkle of mischief back in his eye. "I guess that must be because I was too busy trying to get you to sleep with me?"

Evelyn opened her mouth to give a scorching reply that she knew would have scalded Michael's very ears, but she was interrupted by the sound of someone choking.

Michael and Evelyn both turned to see a very red-looking Samantha trying to hold down her coughs of surprise. She blushed harder when she saw them looking at her.

"I apologize for interrupting you, Mr and Mrs Moskowitz; I was just slightly shocked."

Michael looked baffled at Samantha's words, almost as if she had forgotten she had existed.

"To be continued," he mouthed toward Evelyn, who had to hold back her giggles as they both proceeded to follow Samantha toward the garage.

Michael whistled in awe as the garage door swung open. It was huge! It had enough space for three cars and a separate space for storing garage tools and vehicle parts. Michael pointed out room for Evelyn's Mustang.

"I guess that's enough space for your smart car and my beast?" he asked.

Evelyn hummed in agreement, but Samantha looked slightly lost.

"Smart car and beast?" she asked.

"Oh," Evelyn said, then she laughed slightly. "Those are our cars. We name them."

Samantha laughed, a clear sound that Evelyn thought sounded like the ringing of bells.

"That's an unusual thing to do. But, I like it," Samantha commented.

"Yeah. We are kids at heart," Evelyn informed her.

"Well, I hope you don't mind the neighbors to your left then, the two kids and their father. The father is a doctor, so he is usually out of town, though, so they have a nanny looking after them."

Michael nodded in understanding.

"Woah, we have a doctor living next to us. That is so cool," Evelyn said.

Michael rolled his eyes at her.

"You're a doctor too, Eve," he reminded her, shaking his head a little.

"I'm a chiropractor. He's a *doctor,* doctor," Evelyn said pointedly as if to prove a point. "A *real* doctor."

Michael sighed. "A chiropractor *is* a real doctor, Eve," he argued.

Evelyn was about to retort back, but her eyes fell on a very awkward-looking Samantha trying to look at anything but them, trying not to listen to what they were talking about. Evelyn smothered a chuckle. She and Michael tended to get too involved in their own conversation that they seemed to build an entirely different world around themselves, sometimes. Evelyn was completely aware of this. She stopped and silently hushed Michael, pointing to the blonde girl in explanation.

Michael nodded in understanding and cleverly changed the subject, looking at Samantha and asking, "So, if any of us need medical attention, all we need to do is just check in next door?"

Samantha nodded enthusiastically, relieved she did not have to pretend to have disappeared like she was trying to do before.

"Yes. Yes!" she exclaimed. "And there is a school system as well. It's called K-12. Your children will barely have to walk a block to get to it since it is very near."

"Oh, we, um..." Michael started, looking at Evelyn for help, but she was too busy avoiding his gaze. He knew this was a sore topic for her, and his heart sunk in pain. "We don't have kids," he said quickly as if it would hurt less if he said it faster, like ripping off a band-aid.

"We have two dog babies, though," Evelyn said, recovering slightly, though Michael could still detect a slight shake in her voice. He smiled at her encouragingly.

Roxy and Zeus were pugs. They had wrinkly skin, mischievous faces, and squirming bodies that were unable to sit still for too long. They were always on their next adventure, be it chewing Michael's shoes or hiding under couches. They were extremely chaotic, but both, Michael and Evelyn, loved them to pieces.

"That's excellent then. Because we have a doggy daycare and spa here as well!" Samantha informed them.

Evelyn grinned and said, "That's great. My babies get to have special treatment then. They are going to love it here."

THE NEIGHBORHOOD

"I can't wait to show you the dog room in your house, then," Samantha grinned at them.

"Dog room?" Evelyn asked in bafflement. "But how did you guess we would need one?"

Samantha blanked out for a second, looking as if she had been completely thrown off guard.

"Oh, we build those for everyone and have them remodeled if they don't have a dog," she told Evelyn, but her voice was slightly higher than usual, and her face still held a little hesitation. Then, she quickly turned away, leading them to the living room.

She had been right, there was a little doggy room attached right next to the living room, and its entrance was hidden by a light fabric curtain that camouflaged perfectly with the walls, which were exactly why Evelyn and Michael had missed it in the first place.

"Our little pugs are the best ones! They are absolute little comedians. Those little wrinkles get me every time. But they always get what they want. So, this is just perfect for them!" Evelyn told Samantha, catching hold of Michael's hands, interlocking their fingers together, and squeezing slightly.

Michael squeezed Evelyn's hand in silent response to her excitement, turned his eyes to the roof, and said, in mock dismay,

"Oh lord! Another room for the kids to terrorize."

Evelyn it his arm lightly in jest, knowing he probably barely felt it through the layers of muscle that encased him.

"Oh stop, you," she told him, laughing nonetheless.

Samantha took them back outside, and they noticed that it was already dark. The stars were peeking through the clouds. She noticed the couple looking at the stars and said, "Do you know that a glass dome covers this whole area for your protection?"

Evelyn and Michael both looked slightly baffled.

"Really? But how?" Michael asked.

Samantha laughed, "Don't worry. That is how everyone feels when they first hear about it. It's thin, bullet-proof Japanese glass, fashioned after the famous Glass Bridge model and by the same architect. It is not very famously known, but some classify the glass bridge as the eighth wonder of the world."

"Woah," Evelyn said, still in awe. If she looked closer and was aware of the glass, only then could she see how there seemed to be only a shimmer that indicated something screened the sky. But it was very imperceptible.

"This entire neighborhood also has high walls, lined with camera surveillance and a tightly guarded entrance, so you are completely safe at all times.

THE NEIGHBORHOOD

Furthermore, it has all grocery stores, businesses, stores, food outlets, spas, shopping malls, and even one or two farms, so there is rarely a need to travel too far to purchase things," Samantha informed them.

"Yeah," Michael agreed, turning to Evelyn to tell her, "I did see quite a few shopping malls and bookstores on the way here, including your favorite breadstick-selling food outlet and that one sushi place that we frequently eat. From."

"That's pretty amazing," Evelyn said.

"Well then, I'll take my leave now. Good luck, you guys!" Samantha said, turning to shoot them a brilliant smile before walking away.

"Good night!" Evelyn called out to her. She held out Michael's arm and pulled it over her shoulder, huffing slightly at how heavy it was.

The pair watched Samantha leave, and even long after she was gone, they stood outside in the Maine Autumn warmth, looking up at the sky together.

It was a brilliant night view. They could clearly see all the stars they could not see in the main cities due to the light and air pollution there. Michael was very interested in astrology. He had been a jock in high school and college, but Evelyn often teased him about how he was truly a nerd at heart.

She sunk into Michael's embrace, thinking quietly of her melancholy past and wondering what the future held for them. There was a comfortable silence between the two. They knew they did not necessarily need to speak to convey their thoughts to each other because of the strong connection.

"I think I'm going to like it here," Evelyn whispered to Michael, telling him something she knew he already knew.

Michael smiled down at Evelyn gently. "I think I'm going to like it here, too," he said.

Evelyn and Michael then turned their back on the house, sat in their car, and drove to the home they would soon be leaving behind.

Chapter 4

Growing Up

Evelyn Moskovitz carried herself with a certain grace, borne out of years of practice and years of holding herself up and pretending she was fine even when she was not. As a child, Evelyn had been shy. Not excruciatingly shy, but she was also not a narcissist in the way she believed other girls at her school had been. Because even though she had been a young girl with a quiet, mature vibe, who tried to blend in with the shadows, she had stood out.

Evelyn had long, dark hair that appeared to glow with a lustrous sheen when sunlight fell on them. They seemed to form a halo around her head even when she wore it in the most careless of manners and without much adornment. In the 90s, such dark, long hair was unusual, and so it was a point of both envy and adoration by many of her peers.

Her dark hair was paired with striking green eyes, which were an unusual match for someone with raven black hair. Her eyes tended to shift colors, ranging from deep green to a pale, light blue, or grey, depending on her mood and the colors she wore on a certain day. It often looked as if her eyes themselves were shifting, adapting to suit Evelyn in the best way that they possibly could.

Her skin was a perfect golden tan, one that paled slightly when she was slightly nervous or when she felt cold, but it only further complemented her sharp-featured and angelic looks. Even the way Evelyn talked, with a soft, lilting voice, never failed to mesmerize anyone who looked at her.

Evelyn always had her head in the clouds. She was always dreaming about something or the other, thinking about things that never happened, and creating scenarios that could. Her mind was continuously forming puzzles and fitting them all together, connecting one thing to another, one incident to another. That was also one of the reasons why she was excellent at subjective courses, especially maths.

Evelyn always thought profoundly and felt emotions more deeply and more intensely than most people. She connected her thoughts and expressed them in ways that made people want to stop and listen to her. She made people want to talk to her because of how interested she was in listening to them and their emotions.

Evelyn was an empathy through and through. She was breathtakingly gorgeous, intelligent, and kind, so it was no wonder that most people had been intimidated by her back in her high school. It was also why most of the girls at school had hated her. They had been envious of her looks, of the regal way she carried herself and the way she outsmarted herself.

By the time Evelyn hit high school, she was tired of being ostracized, so she tried her best to fit in with everyone else, and the only way she could think of doing that was by submitting to peer pressure. She began to drink, tried drugs, and started smoking just because everyone else was doing it. For once in her life, she wanted to be 'cool,' but she hated every single moment of it.

She hated every sip of alcohol, the burn of it as it went down her throat, and the bitter aftertaste it left in her mouth. She hated the unbalanced feeling the weed gave her and how it made her cough so hard that her throat often got ripped. She had become the cool girl she had always wanted to be, the one who could fit in with the popular kids, but she had begun to hate herself.

She hated who she had become. She was turning into another clone of the brainless, drug-addicted students that went to her school, and she was helpless to stop it. Finally, she had decided to leave. It was a chance to run, to move away from it all and start again, afresh.

But then there came the call.

It was a Tuesday morning. The sky had been slightly overcast, but Evelyn had been sitting on the porch, twirling a flower between the fingers of her hand absently while she held a book in the other one. She had been trying to catch the last rays of the setting sun while she tried to read to hinder her mind from overthinking. Then, her phone had rang, and it was one of her friends on the line.

"Hey, Eve, you trying out for the cheerleading scholarship this year?" her friend asked.

"Cheerleader scholarship?" Evelyn wondered.

"Yeah. My college has this cheerleading scholarship program for the new freshmen who want to join, and I remembered how you always outperformed me in ballet class," her friend, Saleen, stopped to laugh before she continued. "So I thought of you and figured you should try it out."

"I-" Evelyn said, hesitating slightly. "I'll think about it."

They talked for a while more and then bid each other goodbye.

That phone call was just the chance Evelyn had needed. It was as if some angel was looking down at her from heaven, carving out pathways for her to follow. Evelyn had already been considering running away, but she had been slightly terrified of doing so.

"But what if I go to a college that is far away? Saleen's college. That could work," she mused to herself and then got up to relay her decision to her parents.

Evelyn did not have strict parents. In fact, her parents were more understanding than most, so they happily agreed to let her go to an out-of-state college, even if that meant being apart from their beloved daughter; all that mattered was that it could allow her to recover from the depression she had sunk into.

Her parents had split up when she was only twelve years old, so they lived apart. She was always harangued with questions about who she should stay with, who she should talk to, who she should love more amongst her parents.

People expected her to take sides.

When her parents got divorced, the peer pressure only intensified. Evelyn did not know how she could prove to everyone that yes, she did love her parents equally and no. She did not want to pick who she loved more. It was because she knew that even though her parents disagreed with each other and were unable to love each other, both of them completely and fully loved her.

There were times she wished they could make it work, that they could get along for the sake of their children. But later, as Evelyn had grown up, she had understood their decisions and forgiven them for it. Even then, Evelyn had tried to empathize with her parents and forgive them for their decisions despite all her confusion.

Evelyn had gotten into North-High College, the one where Saleen was, and all that had been left was the try-outs so that she could get the scholarship. That was the daunting part.

When Evelyn got to the try-outs, she immediately stood out. It was as if her problems had chased her all the way to the other side of the state, followed her despite all her efforts to run away from them. It felt like waking up from a nightmare, only to realize that real life was scarier than the nightmare had been. She was singled out again; the spotlight she had tried so hard to run away from was back on her.

When the other girls at the tryouts had seen her in her dark t-shirt, they had scoffed slightly and turned away, adjusting their fancy crop-tops and workout gear. They had immediately labelled her as a 'prude,' already knowing she would not be able to make the cut to be on the team. But Evelyn had worked hard for the try-outs. She had trained herself, and she would not let any blonde-haired, blue-eyed clones of Barbie pull down her self-esteem.

However, despite all her confidence, Evelyn could not help but doubt herself. The cons of being a strong empathy meant that she was never completely indifferent to her emotions, so all the heightened nerves of the girls around her made her feel slightly insecure.

"It's okay, Evelyn," she told herself, trying to drown out

the voice in her head that reminded her that she had only cheered once in her life and that the other girls looked way more experienced.

She had completely shut off her mind while she performed, and then, they waited for the results to be announced. She knew, without certainty, that she had lost. She knew she was not going to be chosen. The other girls had been so much better than she was.

After the try-outs, she turned away, slightly depressed. She turned away, about to leave, when a voice called out, "Merle!"

Merle was her middle name. Whenever she got into trouble, that was the name her parents had shouted out, and her childhood friends quickly caught onto it and started to use it.

"Merle, you got in!" the voice called again, and Evelyn turned to see Saleen.

"I got in?" Evelyn asked incredulously.

"You got it!" Saleen told her, excitedly jumping up and down, overjoyed on Evelyn's behalf.

"No way," Evelyn said. She dashed to the soft board to see that she had, in fact, gotten selected.

'Evelyn Marlene' was printed on the bottom of the list beside the word 'alternate.'

Evelyn squealed in absolute glee, a smile breaking out over her face. She had gotten in. Now all that left between her and the team was if some blonde Barbie accidentally broke her leg.

That night, the day she made the cut for the team, Evelyn had a dream. It was about Melissa, one of the girls on the squad. Evelyn had met her during the try-outs. She had scowled at her and then whispered something to her friends that made them all giggle. Then, she had pointed in Evelyn's direction, and her friends had giggled again.

That was how Evelyn had known Melissa had been mocking her. In the dream, Melissa had been out to a party that Evelyn also happened to be at. Melissa tried to impress one of the jocks, Cole, by doing a backflip. The problem was that she had been too drunk; she fell off a table and broke her leg.

When Evelyn woke up, she shrugged off her dream. She thoughts it was a weird hope that her brain had conjured up. Except, in reality, Evelyn was too kind to ever hope for anyone to break their leg.

The next night, Evelyn got invited to a party over at Cole's house. Cole was the quarterback of the football team. He had stunning good looks, dark hair, blue eyes, and a jawline that could cut through glass. All the girls on the cheer team had a crush on him.

THE NEIGHBORHOOD

Evelyn did not; of course, she did not. She always had her head up in the clouds, daydreaming about anything and everything, to have time to have a crush on that guy that everyone liked. She did think he was cute, and she knew he was smart because he was in the same AP Mathematics class that she was.

He always answered questions quicker than the rest of the class did. He was Evelyn's biggest competitor when it came to their grades. Still, the two maintained a friendly camaraderie, so it was only understandable that Cole would invite her to his party too. What Evelyn did not expect, however, was Melissa to be there as well.

It seemed uncannily similar to her dream.

She frowned when she saw Melissa down shot after shot of vodka and then clumsily stumble up to the kitchen table and attempt to do a backflip off of it. Evelyn gasped when Melissa broke her leg. First, she was concerned, and then confusion took over her concern.

"Why does it feel like my dream is repeating itself?" she asked herself.

She was instated into the cheer team like she had dreamed. In fact, everything had played out exactly as she had dreamed. It was then that Evelyn realized this was not the first time this had happened. Times before this, she had been too young to understand what was going on. Later, when she understood it and told someone about it, everyone passed it off as a déjà vu experience.

Evelyn eventually told Saleen about it, and Saleen was the only one who took her seriously.

"Okay, so, I hadn't fully made the team, and all I had to hope for was that some blonde Barbie broke her leg and I'd be good to go," Evelyn confided to Saleen the day after the accident. They were sitting on the bleachers, watching the football team practice.

"And then I told myself 'as if that would happen,' but it did. Saleen it did. I had just dreamed about it the night before it happened. I don't think Melissa breaking her leg and me dreaming about it was a coincidence. This has happened before."

"Your dream actually materialized? Eve, you're making me think you put a damn hex on this poor girl," Saleen said.

"I know it sounds insane. Heck, I feel as if I have gone completely insane, but I don't know what is happening, and this is not even the first time. It has happened multiple times before," Evelyn said, biting on her lip.

She knew that if anyone believed her, it would be Saleen. Saleen's mother was a fortune-teller. Evelyn had visited her house once and noticed the way it smelled of incense and smoke. She had never believed in fortune, but she had realized, over the years, that Saleen's mother truly was on a whole other psychometric level.

"What?" Saleen asked, shocked. "You've had this happen before?"

"Yeah, what's wrong with me?" Evelyn asked, noting the musing look that came over Saleen's face.

"You know what this means, right?" Saleen started, her voice mysterious.

They looked at each other wide-eyed as if coming to a conclusion, and then, "No clue," they said in unison, their serious facades breaking. Finally, they both dissolved into laughter, the serious mood breaking completely.

"Alright, well, let's make a list," Saleen suggested, regaining her composure, "What dreams you have had that have come true?"

"I'm not sure," Evelyn said, serious now.

"Come on. There has to be another one!" Saleen prompted.

Evelyn thought for a bit, then said, "Well, I did have that dream about Cole and me making out."

"Well, that hasn't happened, damn!" Saleen joked.

"But it could," Evelyn teased back.

"Yeah, yeah, dream on," Saleen said, laughing slightly. Evelyn mock scowled at her but joined in on Saleens's giggles, knowing she was just joking. That was what she liked about their friendship. It was comfortable in a way that allowed them to be themselves with each other.

Eventually, they stopped laughing.

"Well, whatever this is, we need to do some research," Saleen told Evelyn, her brow wrinkled and her blue eyes shining.

"Okay, like how?" Evelyn asked, twirling a strand of hair around her finger like she had seen the rest of the girls do. She decided she liked her dark hair more than she liked the blonde hair everyone else had.

"Books! Library! Hello, it's all free," Saleen said.

"Oh, right, the library is one of my favorite places to drown out all the noise from teenage hell. So let's go after school," Evelyn said.

"Okay, sure. It's open till 5."

Saleen met Evelyn at her locker two hours later. Evelyn had been complaining about the size of the lockers and indignantly questioning how they were supposed to ever fit anything in them, given how cramped they were. It was then that they passed Cole and Evelyn caught sight of him smiling at them.

THE NEIGHBORHOOD

Then his brother came up behind him and smacked him on the head, almost knocking him over. Saleen and Evelyn started laughing at the sight,

It was only when they got to the library and entered it that Saleen asked Evelyn, "What was that?"

"What was what?" Evelyn asked, clueless as always.

"Um, *hello,* he was eyeball screwing you," Saleen said, rolling her eyes jokingly and wriggling her eyebrows.

"No, he wasn't," Evelyn protested. "He just smiled at me."

"Nah uh, missy. He totally has the hots for you. I think another dream is coming true," Saleen said, referring to Evelyn's dream about kissing Cole.

Saleen was right. Another dream was going to come true, but never in a thousand years could Evelyn imagine all the things that were going to take place.

Chapter 5

Devices and Vices

"Babe?" Michael called, glancing over at Evelyn. She was curled up on the couch, like a lithe cat, wrapped up in a fluffy blanket, one hand holding a hot chocolate her Kindle in the other.

"Babe? Eve?" Michael called out to her again.

Evelyn hummed absentmindedly, too engrossed in her book. Michael's face tore into an expression somewhere between adoration and exasperation. He loved his wife; God, he loved her so much, and it was almost impossible to be mad at her because of how adorable she was, but sometimes when she became like this, it tended to get on his nerves slightly.

He really needed help deciding the shipment plans and furniture for their new home, but all Evelyn had done for the past four hours was either stare blankly at the book she was reading or mess around with her phone and browse through old pictures. Sometimes he felt as if she was still living in the past, and he felt impatient with her because she could not move on from it. Then he reminded himself that she had been through more than he could ever imagine and that made him love her all the more.

"You're always on that damn Kindle. I'm going to throw it out the damn window," Michael threatened. He pushed aside the laptop and took a detour to the kitchen to get some food instead.

"I'm sorry, babe, I just-" Evelyn sighed, aware of Michael's frustration. "I just need to fix up my next therapy appointment, and I haven't been feeling the best lately. The dreams are getting worse. More vivid."

Michael looked at her questioningly, and she nodded, "I can't tell what they mean yet, but they're always the same thing, always the accident."

Michael's eyes turned serious and more consoling. He started to walk toward her, but there was a loud pounding from the door.

"Oh crap!" Evelyn exclaimed. "If it's Dale, tell him I'm indisposed."

Michael turned toward the door and then stopped in his tracks, irritation flashing through his eyes.

"You know it wouldn't kill you to be more social, Eve," he jabbed.

"Mike, I *am* social. All day. At the office," Evelyn snapped back at him.

Michael opened his mouth, probably to retort something, but Evelyn shot him a side-eye, and he closed his mouth, looking away. He made his way toward the door.

Evelyn slipped into the bathroom with the Kindle before Dale came in. She really disliked Dale. But then she had a point; Dale had very few likable traits. He was an alcoholic, a single dad, and he cracked nasty jokes.

Nothing that ever came out of his mouth was ever kind or amicable. Instead, it was always laced with a snideness and a lazy drawl to go with it. Nevertheless, Michael was the only one who could tolerate Dale and kept him around, despite her better wishes.

But then again, she felt she wasn't really in a position to tell Michael who he could and could not hang out with. Evelyn usually had an array of excuses at hand just to prevent being in Dale's company. Instead, she heard them talk about the world's many conspiracy theories for the next half an hour.

She had made a cozy impromptu seat for herself in the bathtub, lining it with the many inflatable pillows they had kept, especially for luxurious bathing. She contemplated taking a bubble bath while she waited for Dale to leave, looking longingly at the bath bombs and the scented candles on the shelves but then she figured that she needed to greet Dale.

She held her ear to the door for a minute.

THE NEIGHBORHOOD

Dale and Michael were talking about the coronavirus and how the world was completely in chaos because of it. Evelyn agreed with what they were saying. Covid-19 had completely thrown a wrench in all their plans. The restaurant's opening, the supply buying, her chiropractic clinic, and Michael's projects had all been put on hold during the first wave.

It started up very gradually; the world was still suffering the after-shocks of the virus two years later. Never in her dream could Evelyn have imagined that she would live to see a pandemic, especially one with a magnitude as huge as the coronavirus. They couldn't go anywhere without being announced, scanned, and tested. Grocery shopping had become a thing of the past. Eighty percent of Americans had to *"work from home,"* and childcare was an absolute joke.

Evelyn loved kids; she adored them, and the loss of her own had resounded through her and broken parts of her spirit, but she knew she couldn't imagine having kids or raising them during Covid-19. She always knew they were going to move, but she never thought they would move to a safe-zone neighborhood where they would have to take shooting classes and arms training.

A neighborhood that was like a safe zone, one where residents had background checks done on them before they were admitted, made her feel safe. They were checked for criminal records, DUIs, warnings, restraining orders, and even parking tickets. The only reason Evelyn and Michael had managed to get in was because of their squeaky-clean record.

Both were model citizens, and so they didn't need the extra counseling classes that were mandatory if one had a speeding ticket. The thing she found truly weird was the arms classes, but both, she and Michael, had dismissed it as one of the mandatory requirements needed to keep up with the changing times.

Suddenly Dale pounded roughly on the door. Evelyn took a few steps back and held a hand to her chest. Her lips tilted up into a furious scowl. Things like this made her not like Dale, but that didn't mean she was not going to be civil about it.

"Gorgeous, get out here and say hi to your old buddy, Dale. I heard you made cheesecakes, and I need some to take to the kiddo," the voice at the door called out.

Evelyn rolled her eyes, almost beginning to pray to the heavens for a way out. She just did not like the vibes that Dale had. Being an empath meant she had the ability to sense emotions more keenly and sharply than other people did. She could almost see their aura and feel their feelings.

However, she did not really like the way Dale looked at her or even how he talked to her. His comments were always slightly suggestive, and he always wanted something out of her. In addition, she did not like the aura he exuded.

"Go away, Dale," Evelyn shouted, only half-jokingly. She did not want to be rude, regardless of Dale's aura and the vibes he sent her way.

"No! I refuse," Dale whined.

"Fine," Evelyn said, sighing. "Give me two minutes, and I'll be right out."

Evelyn liked being presentable at all times of the day, so it was understandable that she did not like having sudden guests because she did not like seeing someone without makeup. It was one of the traits she had taken from her mother. She never liked being messy or anything but elegant when she was in the company of other people. Michael was the only exception, and that was because of how comfortable he made her. Everyone else got the perfect side of her.

Evelyn threw open the cupboards, pulled out a tube of lip gloss, applied a dash of some powder over her eyes, and added some pigment to her cheeks, and she was done. She fixed her clothes, tucking her shirt half-in half-out in a deliberately messy, chic look that was recently in style and spritzed on some perfume.

Then she stepped out of the bathroom while pulling her hair into a messy bun. Messy buns were hard to pull off, but Evelyn had long since mastered the art of the perfect messy bun, and it looked absolutely surreal on her. She knew she looked good with a bun because Michael could not stop staring at her when she wore her hair up in one.

She noted, with a satisfied gaze, that Michael was looking her up and down with an open-mouthed expression. She laughed slightly, and then she turned to see Dale giving her a once over and tried to inhibit the frown that she knew was forming on her face.

"Where's my hug, goddess?" Dale asked, holding his arms out wide. Evelyn jokingly side-stepped him, ignoring his arms, simply because she was not comfortable hugging him. She passe it off kindly, though, pretending she did not see them.

"Your hug," she said, teasingly stepping out of his arm's reach. "Is reserved for a time when you need it more. Eve's hugs are rare. You can't just have them whenever you want. It has to be a special occasion."

"Well then," Dale sighed deeply, his beer belly following the movement. "I guess I'll have to wait for that special occasion then."

He winked at Evelyn.

Evelyn caught Michael glaring at Dale and felt slightly gratified. Finally, Michael was starting to see why she was so uncomfortable around Dale.

"Oh my God, Dale!" Evelyn said, her tone joking, hiding her frustration. She flipped him off. Then she wrinkled her nose at herself in disgust. Flipping someone off was something she rarely did, given how crude the gesture was. But Dale made her want to commit homicide sometimes, despite her extremely gentle nature.

"Why are we all so disgusting?" she asked herself.

"Because we have to be professionals during the day, Eve," Michael said, overhearing her.

"Oh, right," Evelyn laughed slightly at his joke.

Michael smiled softly at her, shaking his head at her giggles.

Dale coughed.

"I'm still here, you guys," he protested. "Keep the bedroom eyes for after I get the cake and leave."

"Ah right, I forgot you wanted the cheesecake for Mags," Evelyn said, looking away from Michael as if breaking out of a trance. Mags, short for Margaret, was Dale's teenage daughter. She had blonde hair and green eyes and looked exactly like Dale's ex-girlfriend, her mother. His ex-girlfriend had always been a sort of a psycho. She had dropped Margaret off on Dale's doorstep when she was only a month old. So Dale had to take in Margaret and raise her, all on his own.

Evelyn had to admit that no matter how sleazy and unhygienic of a man Dale was, he was still an incredible father. He memorized all of Mag's likes and dislikes, he kept an eye on her, but he still let her have her space. He was responsible without being overbearing, and Margaret had grown into a very lovely young woman.

She was kind, hated her father's drinking, and was also extremely beautiful. But she was also slightly rebellious, just like almost every other teen was. She had a spirit that was hard to extinguish, one that reminded Evelyn a little of herself. Margaret was also the reason why Evelyn did not completely hate Dale and sympathized with him.

"So, are you staying for dinner? I made some Mexican lasagna last night. We have plenty of leftovers," Evelyn asked Dale, softening ever so slightly.

"Maybe call Mags and tell her to come over?" Evelyn suggested as an afterthought.

"No can do, Goddess," Dale said, shaking his head. "She's out on a date."

"What? With who?" Michael asked, alarmed, making a move as if to get up and look for her.

THE NEIGHBORHOOD

"Calm down, man; it's with someone I've met," Dale reassured him.

Michael tended to be overprotective when it came to the children in his life. He usually treated them as his own kids. However, he was extremely affectionate with Evelyn's nephews and nieces, treating them as if they were his kids. Evelyn smiled at him, finding him adorable.

"Aww aren't you glad we only have to worry about our little pack of barkers, Mike?" Evelyn asked teasingly. She cast a careless look at the dogs, Roxy and Zeus, watching them as they scampered all around the place. They were usually quiet and shy around strangers but very active around Dale, for some reason. It was generally because Dale always interacted with the dogs, playing fetch with them and feeding them under the table.

Evelyn loved the dogs; she really did. They made her melt. But she also had that longing for her own children, specifically the children that she had lost. She tried bringing up the topic of wanting kids with Michael, but he almost always shut her down, preferring not to talk about it and stating that he was not ready to be a father. She did not understand why he felt that way, especially since he was so good with kids.

However, before Michael could reply to her, the screeching sound of a news headline caught all of their attention and drew it toward the television.

"CNN alert! Massive explosions are happening all over Washington DC right now. We are getting word that the President is safely on Air Force One," a newscaster was giving the short brief of what was going on.

Just as the news came on, there was the sound of a gunshot going off outside. The three of the adults in the room jumped, and the dogs barked loudly. Evelyn turned a pale face toward her husband and Dale to see them already looking back at her, equally startled. They knew, right then, that nothing was going to be the same ever again.

Chapter 6

Fight or Flight

Dale stood up from where he was perched on the couch and got his coat. He looked apologetically at Michael and then at Evelyn.

"I wish I could stay longer, you guys, but-" he pointed toward the television. "It's not safe out there, and my sunshine is on a date. I need to go get her."

Michael stood up, his face folded in concern and his brows furrowed.

"I'll go with you," he said, hurrying to put on his shoes.

Evelyn stared in trepidation. She didn't want Michael to go, but she also knew that she should not stop him from going to find Margaret. Dale held up his hands and then rested one of them on Michael's shoulder.

"It's okay, man. It's not safe out. I'll go get my daughter. You get your wife to safety. I'll meet both of you in a few days."

"Will do, man," Michael said. He held out his arms, and

both of them hugged.

"I'm going to head out, you guys," Dale said. He pulled his coat closer around himself and walked out the front door.

"Take care," Evelyn called out to him, and he only nodded his head in response.

Then Dale was gone, the door was closed, and all was silent.

Evelyn and Michael stood in silence for a moment before Michael gestured to the television, and Evelyn unmuted it.

"Bombs continue to fall in Washington DC. Anyone in the downtown area is recommended to evacuate, pack and move out if it is possible. Half of downtown has already been evacuated. It is rumored that the disruption is being caused by radical Trump supporters, more on the news..."

The television kept on blaring, but Michael muted it out.

"Eve, babe, I think we're going to have to move out now. We're going to need into our new home, " Michael said, looking Evelyn in the eye to assert how serious he was.

"I know, but... " Evelyn said, hesitating for a moment, " what about our family, Mike? My parents and my nieces?"

Michael thought for a moment.

THE NEIGHBORHOOD

"Remember my friend, Creed?" He asked.

"Creed? The weirdo with the safe room? That Creed?" Evelyn said, her green eyes lighting up in realization.

Creed was a mutual friend that both Evelyn and Michael had. They had met him at university. Creed had been in the chess club with Evelyn, and it was Evelyn who had introduced him to Michael, so even when she and Creed had fallen out, Michael still occasionally kept in touch with him.

The one thing about Creed was that he had this utter paranoia about pretty much everything. And that was the very reason he had a safe room built under the basement of his house. It had an entrance leading from the basement that went deeper inside. It further led to a government-approved underground escape tunnel that led all the way to Creed's Philadelphia farmhouse. Creed came from a family of government officials and elite business owners, so he was rich enough not to work and still love off his inheritance, afford his mansion, his Philadelphia farmhouse, and get permission for his tunnel.

Creed's safe house had been the brunt of their jokes for the longest time. Everyone teased him about his paranoia, and he always laughed it off good-naturedly. But now it was coming to use.

There was the sound of another sudden gunshot outside

their house.

"That's it. I'm not spending another night here. We need to get out!" Evelyn shouted, slightly hysterical.

Michael nodded at her.

"Calm down, babe. Here..." Michael said, handing her a phone. "You call Samantha and ask her if we can move in tonight or tomorrow at the latest, and I'll call my parents and yours. Then I can call Creed and tell him we're coming over."

Evelyn nodded.

She watched Michael start making his calls. He video called his parents since his mother was hard of hearing, and to talk to her, he needed to use sign language. That was why both Michael and his father were really good at sign language. When Michael's father had met Sarah, Michael's mother, in high school, he had learned sign language just for her. And that was why she married him. Michael automatically learned ASL growing up; it was like his second language.

Evelyn turned away, her hair falling against her cheek as she did so, and walked into the bedroom to make her own calls.

She dialed the number. The phone rang once, twice, and then it went straight to voice mail. Evelyn tapped a foot on the ground impatient as she waited for the beep, after which she could record her message.

"Hey, Samantha- Sammy," Evelyn corrected herself. "I'm glad your voice mail isn't full. Listen, call me as soon as you can. We changed our decision about moving into the house next month."

The phone beeped as the voice mail ended, and Evelyn waited for a bit, starting to pack up the clothes that were still unpacked.

Her phone rang after a few minutes. It was Samantha.

"Hey," Evelyn said, down the phone, dropping the dress she was in the middle of folding.

"Hey, Mrs Moskovitz, I just got your voice mail. Is everything alright?" Samantha said from down the line.

"Yeah. No," Evelyn sighed, flustered.

"Calm down, Evelyn. Are you okay?" Samantha asked, her voice sounding concerned despite the static on the phone.

"Yeah, yeah. Everything is fine. Just... We're going to need to close into the house, Samantha. I know we decided next month, but what with the downtown bombings and the evacuation. We need a place now," Evelyn said, calming herself.

She was usually a very composed woman, but she held a

lot of suppressed trauma that manifested into her panic. She had developed a lot of stress after her miscarriage, and losing the twins had taken a huge toll on her that she was unable to recover from. Losing a child was the most painful thing that could happen to any mother, and Evelyn had lost not one but two of them at the same time. The repercussions of that were traumatizing.

"I understand, Mrs Moskovitz, but we can only provide the house to you by Friday, at the earliest. I'm very sorry," Samantha said. And she did sound regretful that there was nothing she could do.

"It's...that okay," Evelyn said. "We can wait two more days. It's fine."

"Okay, so your punch code to get into the area is 4444," Samantha continued.

'That's odd,' Evelyn thought to herself but did not say it out loud, letting Samantha finish explaining.

"You guys will need to do a retinal scan if you want to get in and then a voice recognition. Once you enter, you need to go to your house. Your house door passcode is 1234, and if you get it wrong more than five times, security will show up," Samantha explained further.

"Okay, wow," Evelyn said. "Anything else?"

"Yeah," Samantha said, and Evelyn could hear her laughing slightly. Her laugh made Evelyn smile too.

"Well, we take your security very seriously, Mrs Moskovitz, hence the cops showing up. But one last thing. The password *1234* is the default passcode. Once you get in, you must change it to your preferred code. Do you have any questions?" Samantha asked.

"Ah no. Thank you for everything, Samantha," Evelyn said politely, meaning every word.

"It's not a worry," Samantha said carelessly. "Thank you for understanding, Mrs Moskovitz. I hope you stay safe. I'll see you soon."

"Bye, Samantha," Evelyn said, then waited till Samantha responded with a hurried *'bye'* of her own before hanging up the phone. She sat down on the bed with a deep sigh.

Two days. Just two more days.

"I hope we can stay safe till then," she said to herself and muttered a quick prayer. "Meanwhile, we are just going to have to move into Creed's house."

Then she tilted her head and said, in a joking voice, "God knows, Creed has enough rooms in that mansion of his to fit five generations of families."

Evelyn shook her head, laughing slightly but also grateful that they had Creed's safe house.

She then called up her work to tell them she was not going to come to work for the next two months, depending on the situation of the city. However, it turned out that the chiropractic clinic itself had been closed temporarily, and hence, all the employees were on leave, so Evelyn was good to go.

She wondered about Michael and his work for a bit, but she reckoned she did not need to worry about it because Michael could handle it. Michael joked around all the time, but he was very smart and quick on his feet when it came to taking action in situations that required his attention. He could also be astonishingly astute when it came to his work and his family's safety. He was the type of person who liked being the family "protector."

Sometimes Evelyn's mother joked about how she and Evelyn's father had hit the jackpot when it came to their son-in-law because of how kind, gentle and loving he was to their daughter.

Just as she was thinking about him, Michael entered the room.

"Hey," he said, "I just called your parents and mine. They have their guns ready for protection, but they are already planning to move into their friends' houses, so we are going to be the only ones moving into Creed's place."

"Oh," Evelyn said. She preferred her family be with her so that she could make sure they were safe and secure, but it could not be helped. She must have subconsciously let a frown take over her face because Michael reached out and smoothed it out.

"No need to stress about, you little worrier," he assured her. "They can look after themselves."

That much was true. Most of her family members were trained in arms usage and trained to use a gun at one point in their lives or another. Her father had been a cop, so he had taught all his daughters to use guns in order to ensure their safety.

"All right. All right," Evelyn said, pulling out of his arms.

"You might want to start packing the rest of the stuff, though," Michael said, glancing around at the haphazard articles of clothing that were also over the place, given that Evelyn had been in the midst of packing when Samantha had called her back.

"Yeah, you're right. Are you done packing your clothes?" she asked him, knowing he would not have.

As she had predicted, Michael sent her a guilty smile, "Nah. I'll get to it right now."

Evelyn laughed and shook her head in absolute adoration. Michael hated packing. He absolutely despised it. In fact, he usually called it the 'bane of his existence.'

While he was still young, Michael's family used to move around a lot because of his father's job. He had changed thirteen schools and two colleges because of that. So, Michael hated packing his things because, to him, the act was connected to the memory of the instability he had to face during his younger days.

He had told Evelyn that it felt like he had had no place, no ground to root himself in. That was, till he had met her. Then, he often confessed that, with Evelyn around, he did not mind moving, especially since he had learned to stop associating home with a place, and he fondly liked telling Evelyn she was his home.

It was slightly cliché in all its entirety, but Evelyn found that she could rarely suppress the cheesy smile that rose on her lips every time he called her that. She felt extremely loved and needed, and it just made her love Michael even more.

She watched as Michael left the room and started packing her belongings. She threw around twenty-five dresses, ten pairs of jeans, sixteen work blouses, two pairs of sweat pants, one tracksuit in around two suitcases. She ran out of space for her purses and her handbags, so she reached into the back of the closet to bring out the bigger one that she and Michael usually took along with them to their vacation destinations.

She put another thirty pairs of heels and ten handbags into

that. Then she pouted, looking longingly at the rest of her clothes and accessories.

"Mike!" she called, but she heard no response.

"Michael," she called again, and he came bundling in.

"Yah?" he asked, then he followed Evelyn's gaze to the wrench in her hand.

"Yeah, I was just making sure the car was in its proper conditions and filled with enough juice to run on," he said by way of explanation.

"Yeah, I did. Can you help me pull these down the stairs?" Evelyn said, pointing to the three huge suitcases.

"Jesus!" Michael whistled and said. "We can come back for your clothes, you know? We're only staying at Creed's place for like, three days at most."

"I know," Evelyn said with a slight pout. "But I need all these clothes with me; I don't feel safe when I'm not with them."

Michael laughed. He had long grown used to Evelyn's shopaholic ways.

"At least it's not drugs," he said, with a smile, echoing the words he had heard Evelyn say every time she bought a new dress for herself when she was at the mall.

Evelyn nodded at his words.

"At least it's not drugs," she said and then smiled.

There was a time when Evelyn was slightly addicted to alcohol, especially after she had lost her babies. But she had a high alcohol tolerance, and she seldom let herself be drunk silly. She was always responsible with it.

"You're absolutely addicted to shopping," Michael mused.

"That I am," Evelyn said as she smirked in response. "But you still love me."

"That I do," Michael said as if it pained him deeply to admit it. He picked up two of the suitcases to take downstairs.

Evelyn laughed loudly at his confession, and he turned, hiding his face, so she did not see him smile. He was glad that, no matter what, he had Evelyn with him to support him through this. She made him smile in a way nobody else ever could.

Chapter 7

School Days

Evelyn's school had an unspoken class system that divided all of us into cliques. There were the jocks, the cheerleaders, the artsy kids, the theatre geeks, and last of all, at the bottom of the hierarchy ladder were the nerds. The nerds were the losers, the ones who were ostracized, bullied by all the rest, and considered inferior.

They barely had any friends and usually sat alone if they ever showed up to the cafeteria, but mostly they just ate lunch in the library or the bathroom stalls. Evelyn was smart, extremely intelligent, and had an impeccable grade record. But she was not one of the nerds. Instead, she was one of the cheerleaders, one of the "cool girls."

It's just that she rarely ever felt that way. She felt as if she was forced under a spotlight, and all lights were on her, especially since she had started gaining popularity. At least amongst the guys. The guys in her school paid attention to her. They liked listening to her speak and hit each other suggestively when she passed them by in the halls.

It made her feel seen, visible, and sometimes it was slightly uncomfortable. But it was this popularity amongst the boys that elevated Evelyn's social status amongst the girls too. The other girls saw her as a threat. She never understood why they felt that way and why they were jealous of her.

Was it because she was prettier than them?

Or because they had heard about Evelyn's singing or her good grades?

Or because they thought she could steal their boyfriend from them?

She did not know why they did that, especially because she really wanted a girl who she could call her friend. Evelyn was shy, not the shyest, by any means, but introverted just enough to not be able to talk to strangers without stuttering or blushing. So, unlike most other kids Evelyn's age, she did not have the courage to just walk up to people and talk to them.

The boys wanted to talk to her. They always hung around her, tried to talk to her, flirted, and tried to ask her out. She could sense it, though. Being an empath meant she could sense precisely what they wanted from her. She could distinguish the ones who just wanted to sleep with her because they thought she was hot from the ones who were truly, genuinely interested in getting to know her more.

THE NEIGHBORHOOD

In that aspect, she was lucky because it meant they were not able to play her. But on the flip side, Evelyn's empath abilities meant that she could also sense the jealousy behind the infuriated glares that the girls sent her way.

Another reason she was popular was that she was the new 'Mystery girl' and everyone wanted to know her. They wanted to know where she came from, why she had shifted and if she was there to stay. It was just that nobody had yet summoned up the courage to ask her about it. That was because of Evelyn's exterior.

She had a hard, outer exterior that screamed, 'Do not mess with me.' It made her seem like a 'cool girl' to others, drawing them to her. The boys thought she was 'hard to get,' which made them want her more. This was why a few girls in Evelyn's class would always make rude remarks about her. They hated her for no reason whatsoever, except that she was smart and beautiful.

"Hey, Morticia! How's it going?" Melanie Cornwall called out to her, deliberately saying Evelyn's name wrong, even though she knew her name. Evelyn knew that she was aware of her name because she sometimes talked about her with her friends while they were in class. And the thing about Melanie was, she could not whisper for shit. So, every time she was talking about Evelyn to her friends, she could hear it.

"You know my name is Evelyn. Don't play dumb," Evelyn

shot back at Melanie, rolling her eyes.

"Oh yeah?" Melanie said. "Too bad you're not memorable enough for me to remember your name."

"And too bad you're too boring for anyone to laugh at your jokes," Evelyn told her. There were slight giggles around the class, and one kid called out, "Roasted!" from the back of the class.

Evelyn laughed slightly and sat on her seat, clutching her binder close to her. She hated Melanie. She was rude to pretty much everyone for no visible reason. Evelyn knew why she was rude to her, though. It was because she was not as generic as Melanie was. She did not have the straight stick body the rest of the cheer team did. She had curves.

She did not have the blonde hair and blue eyes that made them look like a barbie; instead, she had beautiful dark hair and green eyes that shone like emeralds. But most of all, Melanie hated her because she had gotten on the cheer team, and Melanie had not. She felt as if Evelyn had stolen her spot and her dream. But the truth was, she was the one who had not made the cut in the first place.

She was the one who was lagging in all aspects, especially since she was furthest from being athletic or flexible in any way. She cared too much about her extensive fake nails and her glittery clothes to have them be ruined by the excessive exercise cheer practice required. In fact, the only reason Melanie was popular was that she was friends with Colson, the most popular boy in school. The same Cole who had once winked at her from across the hallway while Evelyn was on her way to the library.

The next class was choir. It was Evelyn's first-time attending Honors Choir, and she did not know what to expect. The second she walked in, though, she regretted it. The first person Evelyn's eyes fell on was Melanie, who was giggling in response to something that Cole said to her. She had her hand on his shoulder and was looking at him with infatuated eyes, but Cole turned his head as soon as Evelyn had entered, and his eyes were locked right onto her.

He was not paying attention to Melanie, no matter how much she might have wanted him to. He was staring at Evelyn instead. Melanie noticed that Cole was not looking at her. She followed his line of sight, and her gaze fell on Evelyn. Her lips twisted up into an ugly scowl, and Evelyn winced, looking away.

"Great!" Evelyn said to herself quietly, making sure that nobody else heard her. "The bimbo and her boy toy are both in this class."

Except Cole was not her boy toy. Far from it. Colson and his twin, Cameron, were the notorious duo of fraternal twins who dominated the high school. If anything, it was more plausible that

Melanie was one of their side-chicks instead of the other way around.

Evelyn picked a seat away from the two of them at the front of the class. She hated sitting at the front and almost always sat at the back, but the choir teacher in her previous school had a habit of getting her to come to the front of the class to demonstrate the versatile pitch Evelyn's voice had. So, she figured it would be the same in the new school and, for ease of mobility, she decided to pick a seat closer to the front.

For some reason, Melanie shifted seats soon after Evelyn had taken hers and sat right behind her. She did not think much of it. Melanie was not the kind of person Evelyn would ever be intimidated by. She sensed that Melanie's bullying tendencies arose from deep-rooted insecurities within herself and was determined not to let her get to her. Melanie fidgeted behind her, but the class had begun, so Evelyn did not turn to look.

It was only when class was over that she understood what Melanie had been doing. She had stuck Evelyn's hair, Evelyn's beautiful brunette locks, to the desk with a wad of gum. Evelyn did not want to make a scene and allow everyone to witness her humiliation. However, she was aware that Melanie had taken out a camera and started to record her, so she did not even make any odd faces.

THE NEIGHBORHOOD

When she noticed her hair stuck to the desk, all she did was tug at it. Finally, when she could not free herself, she pulled out a pair of scissors that she carried on her for art class and calmly cut off the part of her hair that was stuck to the desk. She knew that she would never, not in a million years, allow Melanie to see how truly panicked she had been.

Then she pulled the wristband she had off of her wrist and tied her hair up in a bun so that the cut-off part was not extremely obvious. The next day, she had her hair cut short, but she did not mind that because the new shorter haircut emphasized the prominent bone structure of Evelyn's face, drawing attention to her high nose and sharp cheekbones.

Another thing that Evelyn hated about high school was how awful the other children were. High school is made up of a majority of fifteen- to sixteen-year-olds, most of whom have not yet grown out of their immature, spoilt brat phase and tend to poke fun at anything that is even slightly odd. Melanie had blonde, almost white hair. And her skin was tanner than anybody else's, so she was already meeting the classic yet cliché, American beauty standards. Unfortunately, Evelyn did not meet that standard.

But what was worse was the way her mother drove her to and from school in a Porsche. Evelyn was well aware of the way her mother picked her up in a bright purple car. That car was her mother's baby. She had a million different stickers stuck on its bumper, making it stand out from other cars.

Evelyn hated that car.

She really did.

She knew that the other kids in school had seen the car and silently made fun of it. Evelyn really did love her mother, and she was very grateful that her mother usually picked her up from school, so she didn't have to take the bus, but, at the same time, she was embarrassed about her mother's car and the comments the other teens made about it.

They called it "retro and old-fashioned."

They commented on how her mother's car looked like a news reporter's van, with all its many stickers. They said she was too poor to afford a real car, and Evelyn tried to pay no heed to them, but sometimes comments like these affected her greatly. She did not want to be known as the *"girl with the embarrassing mother."*

She wanted to move on and be liked. She wanted friends. She had days where she hid in the library, under the table, so that she did not have to spend her free blocks in the cafeteria. Other days, she used to hide in the stalls in the toilet to have lunch silently. It got so bad that she did not feel like going to school most

THE NEIGHBORHOOD

days.

The insecurities would creep up on her. She realized how her mother and her siblings were the epitome of beauty, but she fell short with her chubby cheeks and short hair. So she felt she was ugly, even though she was not. It was because of that that she developed an eating disorder. It was later diagnosed as bulimia by the school counselor.

The only interesting thing about her high school was the twins Colson and Cameron. They were both exact copies of each other with similar dark hair and dark eyes. Both of them were blessed with beautiful tan skin, a set of pearly teeth, and a nice smile. But they could not be more different when it came to their personalities.

Cameron was the player. He had piercings, wore his hair up in spikes, had a tattoo on his left middle finger, and always had a girl handing off his arm. He was notorious for having slept with all the popular girls, yet, women still wanted him. They wanted him because they believed they could change him.

Colson, on the other hand, was more down-to-Earth. He wore his hair down in loose waves, did not have piercings, and usually wore oxford shoes and fluffy sweaters that made him look soft and almost cute if it were not for his muscles. And for some reason, both of them took an interest in Evelyn.

Chapter 8

Troys' Oyster Bar

A few days later, Michael and Evelyn moved into their new house. Shifting was complete within under a week; it took another week for them to settle in fully. It was only after that that the neighbors started dropping in, one after the other, with piles of freshly baked cookies as welcome gifts. By the end of that third week, Evelyn was running out of space in her fridge because it was fully stacked with the homemade delicacies that her neighbors kept bringing over.

For some reason, all of them liked Evelyn and Michael. They unanimously decided to consider them as one of their own. Evelyn smiled slightly as she thought about how friendly the neighbors were.

Back in their previous area, the neighbors had never been particularly friendly or even inclined to talk to Evelyn much. They were aware that Evelyn and Michael were a couple, way past their prime, in their forties, and they still did not have any kids. To the neighbors, it was a sort of red flag.

THE NEIGHBORHOOD

So, Evelyn and Michael were mostly never invited to the parent activities, the park excursions, the picnics, and the birthday parties. Evelyn remembered when all the mothers had formed a Poetry Club together, but none of them had invited her. In fact, the only way she had found out about it was when Mrs Smith, the neighborhood *'gossip-lady,'* had accidentally blurted it out to her.

She remembered watching the neighbor's lawn across from them cluttered with huge pink jumpy castle, chocolate fountains, and kids' toys. That day, it seemed as if the entire neighborhood had gathered there - all of the women and all their kids. Yet, Evelyn had not been invited. She had been completely excluded.

She had wanted to shout at them, to tell them she was not broken, and they should stop looking at her like there was something wrong with her. Their looks and shifting glances only made her blame herself for losing her twins. She had started to feel suffocated under the burden of their stares and the guilt she harbored because part of her wondered if the miscarriage had been her fault. Rationally, she knew it was not her fault; of course, she did. But the way the other women treated her made her feel like it was.

She was glad she was finally away from the toxic negativity that her old neighborhood provided, and she was pleased that things were looking up. Then, a knock on the door broke Evelyn out of her musings. She walked over to the front door and peeked out from the peephole in the door. It was Samantha. She opened the door and ushered the younger woman inside.

Samantha stepped over the threshold and then stopped, looking around.

"You really have set this space up, beautifully!" she exclaimed.

Evelyn blushed at the compliment.

"Thank you. I chose the furniture, and Michael picked the mahogany floor finishing and the wall paintings."

"It's spectacular," Samantha gushed, taking a seat at the sofa Evelyn had gestured to. Evelyn was just beginning to wonder why Samantha had dropped by when she spoke up.

"Ah, Evelyn, I'm glad to have caught you on your day off. The thing is, a few of us are gathering at Troys' Oyster Bar as an attempt just to catch up since it has been quite a while. It is going to be at eight. We'd love to see you and Michael there."

Evelyn paused for a bit.

"Yes," she said, "Of course, I'll be there. Michael and I will both be there."

Evelyn smiled at Samantha, who smiled back at her.

"Well," Samantha muttered. "I'd best be off," she gathered her coat before Evelyn could protest or ask Samantha if she wanted to stay for tea. Once the door had closed behind her, Evelyn smiled to herself.

"Yeah," she said to herself. "I'm glad we moved into this neighborhood."

***

Michael and Evelyn stood at the entrance of the Troys' Oyster Bar. Evelyn was wearing a dark green dress that set off the green in her eyes and the natural dark highlights in her hair. Michael wore a dark button-down, with a green tie, to compliment her dress.

Evelyn chewed at her nails.

Michael scowled and pulled her away from her mouth, holding it in his own.

"You don't need to be nervous, babe. You'll do fine!" he assured her.

Evelyn smiled weakly at him as they both walked in. They spotted Samantha as soon as they entered, and she waved them over. They sat at the table, and Evelyn set down her purse. There were five other people at the table, two men and three women, including Samantha.

Samantha first introduced them to Daniel and Gracie Smith. They were an older couple, somewhere in their sixties, and their kids had long moved out of their house. The other two people at the table were Pearl and Evan Childers.

They all started ordering their drinks. Evelyn noticed how everyone else was ordering Troy's famous oysters. She hesitated for a bit. It was eight-thirty in the night, and oysters were known for their high protein content. She knew that she would probably be too energetic to sleep all night if she had some now. Evelyn had a higher metabolism than most people did, so she digested foods faster and managed to maintain the body of a twenty-year-old, despite being forty. But one downside of her quick metabolism was that she had to watch what she ate because certain foods could cause her to stay awake at night. She started fidgeting with her hands, wondering if she should order some.

'Oh, what the heck?" Evelyn muttered under her breath. "Let's go for it."

She ordered her share of oysters and waited anticipatingly while the rest of them talked. She zoned into the conversation when she heard her name.

"Evelyn?" Michal asked. She turned to look at him, and he gestured to Pearl. "She asked you a question."

"Huh?" Evelyn smiled guiltily. "Sorry. I zoned out. What

did you ask?"

Pearl laughed good-naturedly and then said, "It's all okay. I was wondering what your choice of poison was?"

"Oh," Evelyn said, then mused for a bit, wondering what her favorite alcoholic drink was, then she shot a wink at Pearl and said, "Whisky, straight."

"Ooooh," Samantha cheered. "Not a soft drinker, are you?"

"Nope," Evelyn told them, slightly proud of how well she could hold her liquor. "It's all or nothing for me," she continued with a daredevil grin.

"So, are you going to drink tonight? We are all planning to get drunk, granted that this one," Grace stopped, nudged her husband. "This one does not drink all that much because he is going to be the designated driver tonight."

Evelyn whooped, letting go of any inhibitions she had previously harbored.

"I'm in!" she cheered. "Let's get shitfaced tonight!"

Michael winced. He was low key terrified of the way Evelyn could get when she was drunk. But at the same time, drunk Evelyn could be insanely endearing. It was the only time she ever let him be the macho man and take care of her. She was always so strong. It was only when she was drunk that she let her walls down slightly.

Their oysters came as the topic of discussion shifted to kids. The premonition Evelyn had come back to her, and she fidgeted in her seat. Michael sensed her unease and wound a hand around her shoulder, pulling her closer to him. He knew she was slightly apprehensive about the discussion and prayed that nobody would ask her about it.

After twenty years of being married, Michael had learned to recognize exactly what Evelyn was feeling and guess some of her thought processes. He pulled her closer and dropped his head to her ears.

"Relax," he whispered.

Suddenly, Evan looked at them and whistled.

"Get a room, you two," he announced, catching everyone else's attention. He teasingly pulled on a disgusted expression and then laughed along with everyone else.

Evelyn blushed and made a move to free herself, but Michael refused to relinquish his hold on her.

"Yo, don't blame me for being in love and having a beautiful wife," he told Evan, his blue eyes twinkling with mirth.

"I won't, man. Of course, I won't," Evan said, raising his hands.

"By the way, do the two of you have kids?" Daniel asked. Gracie nodded along with him.

Panic rose in Evelyn's chest, but she tapped it down as much as possible. Just then, the waiter interrupted them. He placed their dish of oysters at the table, and conversation halted for a while. Evelyn sighed in mild relief as everyone turned their attention to the food.

The conversation rose back up.

"So?" Gracie asked expectantly.

"No, we, uh-" Michael said, answering Gracie. "We don't have kids."

He glanced at Evelyn to make sure she was okay. Pearl glimpsed Evelyn's pale face, understood that the topic was sensitive for her, and shifted the attention to herself to give Evelyn room to breathe.

"We don't have kids either," Pearl quickly said, gesturing to herself and Evan. "We adopted the daughter of my sister after she, um," Pearl stopped to clear the emotion from her voice before she continued. "And now we raise her. We named her Teal."

Evelyn smiled slightly, grateful that the attention was finally off of her. She shot a grateful smile at Pearl, who returned it with one of her own. She then noticed Gracie looking at them both with narrowed eyes. In order to calm her nerves, Evelyn picked up an oyster, almost exactly at the same time Samantha did, too.

They both smiled at each other and then clinked oyster shells together. Evelyn threw back her throat and gulped hers down the throat. It did not taste bad, not really. She just thought it was too overrated. It tasted slightly slimy. Evelyn giggled quietly when she thought of how oysters were reputed for being an expensive delicacy and doubled down as excellent aphrodisiac. To her, they just seemed untasteful and slightly disgusting. She was grateful she had also ordered her usual King Crab. She downed the oyster with a drink of her margarita.

There was a shout of surprise at the back of the diner, and all of them turned to look. One of the customers had stumbled into a waiter, sending a tray of hot oysters crashing to the floor. The waiter hastily collected the fallen oysters.

"I'm so sorry, everyone," he said, flashing a huge smile at the customers looking at him. He was huge, built like a wrestler.

"He looks like Jason Mamoa's brother," Michael joked, but Evelyn felt too sick, all of a sudden, to laugh at his joke.

The waiter was finally done collecting the oysters, and he stood up straight.

THE NEIGHBORHOOD

"Ah yes. You haven't been to Troys' if you haven't witnessed a near-death experience," chimed the waiter, good-naturedly. It was an inside joke that the customers shared, but Michael and Evelyn were new. Gracie started explaining it to them, but Evelyn could not concentrate on her voice.

Evelyn's vision blurred in and out of focus, and her mind echoed the words, *"Near-death experience."*

Her breathing got shallower, and she bleakly wondered if she had a panic attack. She felt as if she was dying. Her throat was closing up, and she gasped for air, holding a hand up to her throat. She tried to scream, but she could barely utter a word.

At first, Michael thought she was just snuggling deeper into his arms, but then he looked down at her when she didn't stop wriggling around. He noticed, with panic, the way she had turned pale, so pale that a light shade of blue-tinged her cheeks. She was literally turning blue in the face. Michael panicked. He stood up and tried to get Evelyn to drink water, patting her back to get her to breathe. Pearl yelled at everyone to call 911, pulling out her phone to do the same.

The panic only made Evelyn's condition worse. She felt dark spots dance in front of her vision, getting darker and darker till her vision faded completely, and then, her mind shut off.

She did not know what happened after that.

Chapter 9

The Hospital

Beep. Beep. Beep.

The sound of the heart monitor echoed in the tiled hospital room. Evelyn had started waking up from her subconscious state. She could feel the warmth behind the closed lids of her eyes, and someone was holding her hand in theirs. She tried moving her hands, only managing to get her fingers to move weakly.

There was a gasp, and the hand that held her tightened on her fingers. There was movement, and then Evelyn heard the beep of a button. It sounded like the one on the side of the bed that's used to call a nurse.

"Evelyn," a voice called out, one that she identified as Michael's. "Open your eyes, Evelyn."

Evelyn tried to do what Michael said, and it took a while for her to open her eyes since she found that she barely had the energy to breathe. However, she managed to do so, wincing when the fluorescent hospital lights flooded her vision.

"That's it, babe," Michael talked her through it. She saw

him smiling widely as she managed to open her eyes fully and look at him. She opened her mouth to say something, but no sound came out. Michael used his other hand to pour a glass of water. He brought it to her lips and watched as she gulped it down greedily.

"More?" he asked.

Evelyn shook her head. Michael had barely set the glass back on the table before the nurse came bustling in.

"Ah, Mrs Moskovitz. I'm glad to see you're awake," she said, smiling brightly.

"Wha-"

Evelyn tried to speak, but her voice broke off halfway. She tried again, clearing her throat and laboriously pronouncing the words.

"What happened to me?" she asked in a soft, whispery voice.

The nurse smiled sympathetically and said, "Shellfish allergies."

Evelyn paused for a bit, thinking.

"Shellfish allergies?" she asked, her voice slightly louder than a whisper but still weak.

"Yes," Michael said with a nod. "Turns out you're allergic

to oysters. Jesus, how could you not know that Eve?" He ran one hand frustratedly through his hair, raking it away from his face.

Evelyn said nothing, looking away. She had no idea she had any allergies, much fewer shellfish allergies. She had never tried oysters before, so they had never found out. She ground and hid her face under the blanket.

"Do you know how worried I was?" Michael sighed. "You gave me a fright."

"Well, I'm sorry. I have shellfish allergies, and I didn't know," Evelyn said, snark clear in her voice. "Am I supposed to apologize for fainting, too?"

"No, it's not-" Michael began saying but then stopped, sighed, and then breathed deeply before continuing. "You're right. I'm just projecting my worry as anger and misplacing it on you."

He smiled down at her.

Evelyn pulled her head back out of the blanket, and when she looked at him, her eyes held no judgment.

"I know. I just wanted to make you realize that," she said.

One of the reasons that they had managed to stay together for so long was because of how much they respected each other. Both of them could take a step back from an argument, maturely analyze their own emotions and talk about what they were feeling.

THE NEIGHBORHOOD

It was also why they connected so well. As if they had a soulmate connection that allowed them to understand each other, even without words.

Evelyn managed to sit up, and it was only then that Michael told her.

"Hey, there was another person who got an allergic reaction at the same time you did."

"Who?" Evelyn asked him.

"This child on the other table. The one we met briefly in the bar before his nanny took him away to the other table. I think his name was Christian."

"Oh!" Evelyn said, eyes lighting up in realization. "Is he okay?"

"I don't know, but-" Michael began saying, but there was a knock on the door, and a younger woman in her early thirties walked in.

"Is the child staying in room 201, Christian Thomas, your son?"

Evelyn felt a pang of pain in her heart. She and Michael looked at each other, and Evelyn's memories came back to her. She remembered being introduced to two children who looked so alike she assumed they were twins, but she did not think it was polite to ask them. She remembered having a short conversation with the girl, Bailey, and automatically taking a liking to her.

The alcohol she had been drinking had dulled the memory of meeting the kids and their nanny. She started putting bits and pieces of her memory together. Suddenly, she wanted to see how Christian was doing. There was this instinct within her that wanted her to check on him, and it was tugging at her empath spirit. She felt like this was something important.

"No," Michael told the nurse. "But can we visit him?"

"I'm sorry, sir," the nurse said, looking at him sympathetically. "Only the relatives of the patient are allowed visitation rights."

"I'm his mother," Evelyn blurted out. She had no idea why she did that, but it felt like the right thing to say. Even now, as the hollow feeling in her chest grew, she did not regret saying that."

The nurse squinted her eyes at Evelyn and looked at Michael in question.

"He's my son, not my husband's," Evelyn explained simply, the lie slipping from her lips so fluently she almost made herself believe it was true. In fact, it was true; Evelyn just didn't know it then. Michael nodded in response to Evelyn, understanding what she was trying to do from the connection they shared. This way, the nurse had no choice but to let her visit Christian.

THE NEIGHBORHOOD

"Fine. This way, ma'am," the nurse said, somehow relenting all of a sudden.

Evelyn tested her limbs, sitting up and then standing up. She looked at the nurse with squinted eyes and said, "It's fine. I'll find my way there."

The nurse obliged and left. Evelyn changed out of the hospital gown, took a quick warm shower, and changed into the clothes that Michael had gotten for her. Then she took Michael's hand in hers, and they both walked, hand in hand, to see how Christian was faring.

They found door number 201, knocked, and entered. Christian was a handsome boy of sixteen. Evelyn reckoned he was popular at school. He was sprawled across the hospital bed, sitting up slightly and trying to find the remote to the television mounted on the wall in order to turn it off. The noise was grating on him.

He turned when Evelyn and Michael entered the room, but instead of being surprised, he just smiled at them, almost as if he expected that they would be there. Evelyn felt something was weird, but then he turned to look at her; she felt an overwhelming feeling of protectiveness for the young boy.

"Hey Christian, do you remember us?" Michael asked him.

"Yup," Christian nodded, finally wrestling out the remote

from between the complicated folds in his blanket. "Michael and Evelyn, right?"

"Yeah, that's right," Evelyn said, taking in Christian's messy dark hair and green eye that bordered on blue. For some reason, he looked very familiar, but she just couldn't put the finger on what it was that made her think that way. She did note that his eyes were a unique, clear green color that looked a little similar to her own eyes. She shook it off as a coincidence and reasoned that a lot of people had green eyes.

"Where's your nanny?" Michael asked him.

"Oh, she's dropping my sister, Bailey, off at home. But she did tell me that the two of you would be coming around," Christian informed them.

"Huh?" Evelyn said, then looked at Michael.

Michael nodded and said, "Yeah, I texted their nanny, Dora, while you were in the shower. She must have told him."

Evelyn nodded.

"So, Chris…" she started but then hesitated, backtracking, and asked. "Can I call you Chris?"

Christian held Evelyn's eyes, staring at her for a moment as if wanting to tell her something. But then he shook his head, closed his eyes before opening them, and said, in a steady voice,

"My mother used to call me Chris. She died when I was still very young."

"I-," Evelyn stuttered. "I'm sorry. I'll just call you Christian," she quickly amended.

"No, no. It's fine," Christian said, smiling softly at her. "You can call me Chris. I like it. It sounds right coming from you."

Evelyn went, "awwww" at his response.

Michael playfully narrowed his eyes at Christian.

"You flirting with my wife, little buddy?" he joked.

Christian smiled at him and began to say something, but then he was interrupted by the door opening. Christian's nanny, Dora, bustled in. She was an older woman in her seventies, with rapidly greying air, but she still looked elegant somehow, a little like Miranda Cosgrove.

"Thank you for looking after this little one while I was dropping Bailey off at home," she told Michael and Evelyn.

"Ah, we wanted to visit him anyways. It's fine," Michael waved off her gratitude. It really was not a big deal, especially since he could see that, for some reason, Evelyn was already attached to the children.

"Where's their father?" Evelyn asked Dora.

"Oh, Mr. Thomas is almost always away on business. He is predominantly located in the international industry, so he is usually traveling and isn't home a lot," Dora said, by way of explanation.

Evelyn turned back to Christian and asked, "So, you did not know you had a shellfish allergy either?"

Christian shook his head and said, "Nope. I didn't even taste it. All it tasted like, to me, was heat and salt."

Evelyn furrowed her eyebrows, and Dora began to cough loudly in the background as if trying to distract Evelyn, but Evelyn had already heard what Christian had said, "Heat and sa-"

Christian quickly interrupted her, blurting out, "Because it was spicy, you know? Spicy for me. It tasted slightly disgusting, like warm flesh."

Evelyn did not buy it, but she let it go. She sensed it was something that Christian was trying to hide from her, but for some reason, her intuition told her that he was not a bad child.

"Ah. I found it disgusting, too," she said.

"Yup. Never eating oysters again," Christian said in response.

"Definitely," Evelyn chimed.

Then both of them looked at each other and started to

laugh. They had a very similar sense of humor, and they had already bonded.

***

"Phase one, part six: establish a connection with Evelyn. Accomplished," Christian typed out on his phone, sending a quick message to Bailey, making sure that neither Evelyn nor Michael accidentally read the text.

He would have used the telepathy link that he and Bailey shared, but sometimes he liked typing on his phone. It was refreshing doing things the way humans did it.

Christian and Bailey were both half-human, half-angel beings who had never lived on Earth before. So, it was fun discovering all the things that they could and could not do. One thing they definitely knew they couldn't do, was taste human food.

Angels do not need food.

So, it was not surprising that they could not taste food since they had no need to. But if the twins wanted to blend in with their surroundings, they had to pretend that they could taste the food. They both went to a special school within the area, one specifically constructed to teach young angels to blend in with humans.

Evelyn had told the nurse that she was Christian's mother. What she did not know, however, was that it was true. Christian and Bailey were the twin fetus siblings that had died even before they were born. Evelyn had been pregnant with them when she miscarried, and the children were innocent enough to get to heaven.

They had grown up in heaven, trained there, and learned there till it was time to be put back on Earth. God had placed the twins on Earth to guide Michael, and especially Evelyn, out of their depression and the unfulfilled feeling that they had.

"Commencing phase two," Christian muttered to himself, watching Evelyn and Michael talk to each other. He twisted his wrist in a circular gesture (angels did not need words to communicate. They could simply converse through ambiguous gestures. It was a language they had created for themselves), trying to get his nanny to put the plan into action.

***

Dora nodded at Michael, and they stepped in to get Evelyn and Michael's attention.

"Hey," she said. "So, we are having a pool party on Friday. I would love it if you guys were there, too."

Evelyn hesitated. This was the first time they had been invited by one of their neighbors, and she did not accidentally want to make a bad impression on them. She was even slightly nervous.

But Michael was confident.

"Friday?" he asked.

"Yes. On Friday," Dora confirmed. Evelyn looked at Dora and her dark, trustworthy eyes. There was something very comforting about Dora. Evelyn knew Dora was non-judgmental and that she could trust her.

When Evelyn spoke, her voice was decided and confident.

"Friday it is then," she affirmed with a soft smile. "We'll be there."

Chapter 10

The Party

The pool party was in full swing by the time Michael and Evelyn showed up. It was extremely impressive. There was a small blue and white jumping castle off to the side for the younger kids. The pool was filled to the brim with clear water, and the crisp smell of the barbeque meat permeated the space.

Evelyn looked skeptically at some of the garden dwarves that were placed strategically around the yard. She was dressed in a flowy, wine-colored sundress, one that fell to her knees and was accentuated by peach ballet flats. Evelyn rarely ever wore heels. She just felt that heels weren't practical enough to walk in. Michael was dressed in a casual white tee and a pair of jeans. In Evelyn's opinion, they both looked fabulous.

Evelyn's green eyes fell upon the couple waving to them across the yard. It was Kenna and Kyle, the couple who were the original hosts of the party. Michael offered Evelyn his arm and led her toward them. Kenna was dressed simply in a blue sheath dress, a stark contrast to Evelyn's wine red one. She looked stunning.

"Hello!" Evelyn exclaimed upon reaching the couple.

"Hey, Evelyn. How are you doing today? And who's this?" Kenna asked, nodding her head in Michael's direction.

Evelyn laughed slightly.

"I'm doing great," she said and then moved Michael slightly in front of her, "And this is my other half. This is my husband, Michael Moskovitz."

"Oh, hey," Kyle said, in a voice deeper than either Evelyn or Michael had expected. He extended his arm toward Michael and waited for him to grasp it.

"Nice to meet you, Michael. I'm Kyle."

Michael broke out into a smile and took the other man's hand. They shook and then stepped back. Evelyn shrugged at their little exchange, caught Kenna's eye, and then laughed.

Kenna pointed to one of the children in the yard.

"See him?" she asked, gesturing to a boy with a pointy nose and a shock of dark hair.

"Yes?" Evelyn said with a slight nod of her head.

"That's our son, Charlie. He's turning thirteen today. They grow up so fast," Kenna said.

"Oh," Evelyn said, a bit awkwardly, then she shook her

head. "I don't really have children."

Surprisingly, Kenna just smiled when she heard Evelyn's response.

"Oh, Charlie isn't our biological son, of course," she said. "We look nothing alike, after all. He's adopted."

Evelyn looked closer and noticed Kenna was right. They did look nothing alike. Charlie had a shock of brown hair while both Kenna and Kyle were red-haired. They both had extremely pale skin, while Charlie was slightly darker and more tanned.

Evelyn marveled at Kenna's ability to talk about her lack of children so easily when it was something that still choked her up, even fifteen years after her miscarriage. Evelyn still felt a hard lump settle in her throat whenever anybody brought up the topic of children. It was one of the things she felt worst about.

She felt as if she was lacking as a woman. She felt this deep hold in her heart because she did not have anyone to love, care for, and adore except Michael. She was acutely aware that the absence of kids from her life and her miscarriage had made her feel hollow and driven her into a mild depression.

She smiled at Kenna and noticed Michael looking down at her with a concerned expression.

"Hey," Michael nudged Evelyn slightly. "You, okay?"

"Yeah," Evelyn said, coughing slightly. "I just-"

"It's okay," Michael said before quietly escorting her away from Kyle and Kenna.

That was when Evelyn's eyes fell upon Bailey. She was looking away from them, turned slightly inward, toward the door. She was holding her phone in both her hands, typing away rapidly on the screen of her iPhone. Her eyes seemed to glimmer like stars, and there was a small smile on her lips.

She kept trying to bite her lips to stop the smile from creeping up, but Evelyn noticed it anyways.

"I guess she's talking to a boy," Evelyn said, with a slightly teasing smile in her voice, pointing it out to Michael.

Michael looked at Bailey and scowled slightly.

"Isn't she slightly young to have a boyfriend right now?"

Evelyn hit him on the arm.

"She's sixteen, Mike," she protested. "Besides, it's her father who is supposed to be worried about her, not us. So why do you care?"

Evelyn cared too. In fact, she cared so much about the twins, for no plausible reason, that she was confused and overwhelmed by her own emotions. She did not understand why she felt the urge to look after the kids. She felt connected to them as if they belonged to her.

"I don't know," Michael told her in response. "But for some reason, both those kids trigger a protective instinct within me. I think it comes from your empath skills, Evelyn."

Evelyn scowled up at him. But she knew he was right. Her empath skills did tend to affect Michael. She had always believed they had a soulmate bond, and maybe that was why he had caught some of her talents.

Evelyn was an empath which meant that energy was like a wave to her. She could sense the transfer of it from one person or form to another.

It was harder for her to be in large crowds because she tended to absorb all energy around her like a magnet. Sometimes it was hard to tell if her feelings were her own or just something seeping over into her aura from another person's projections.

So, when normal people felt something strong, she, in comparison, felt it a hundred times more strongly. Evelyn was gifted, but she was still developing her gifts. She had dreams that guided her. Recently, though, her dreams had centered around major accidents and catastrophes.

So, she decided it was time to move across the country

without convincing her husband first, hence their move to their new place. But sometimes, when she was closest to someone, or she had that connection with them, she tended to transfer her energy to them, as in the case of Michael.

Evelyn saw Samantha and waved her over. Unlike every other time, though, Samantha was not alone. She was holding the arm of a blonde-haired, blue-eyed surfer guy. The both of them smiled as they moved toward Evelyn and Michael. Evelyn pulled Samantha into a hug and thanked her. Evelyn was a soft, gentlewoman. She tended to feel deeply because of her empathy and get attached to people faster. Samantha was already like a younger sister to Evelyn.

"How have you been doing, Sam?" she asked.

Samantha twirled around to show off her plain grey dress and then laughed slightly.

"I swapped my professional outfit for this one, so I guess I am doing good," she said.

She nudged the arms of the man she was with and smiled politely at Michael, then said, "This is Ryan. He's my brother."

Ryan nodded his head at Michael and Evelyn with a slight smile before excusing himself. Samantha grimaced as he walked away.

"He's so antisocial," she complained to them. "He spends all his time at the beach lagoon area, surfing his days away. I thought maybe getting him to come here would allow him to interact more, but he is acting like he hasn't had any orbs in years."

"Orbs?" Evelyn asked Samantha, and for a second, Samantha blanked out, then she coughed.

"Food," Samantha said, her voice coming out weak. She cleared her throat and then said, "Food" again, in a stronger voice this time.

"Oh, I thought you had said 'orbs' for a second there, and I was confused," Evelyn said, meeting eyes with Michael, who looked equally as confused because he could have sworn that he had heard Samantha say the word 'orbs.'

Samantha blushed and looked away before starting to change the topic.

"Look at Christian showing off his smooth pool dives," she said.

Michael watched for a moment before he spoke up.

"Where is the children's father?" he asked Samantha.

Samantha's face softened slightly while she thought of their father, and Evelyn sensed that Samantha probably harbored feelings for him.

"The children's father," Samantha sighed. "Is a doctor. So, he is currently abroad, trying to find a cure for COVID-19."

"Oh, that is amazing!" Michael said. "But don't you think the children need some guidance. We just saw Bailey talking to some boy or another, and I just feel like making sure that nobody would harm her or take advantage of her naivete."

Michael looked away in slight contemplation before focusing back on Samantha, "When is he coming back?"

Samantha sighed and said, "Doctor Phillips has been away for the past two years. None of us knows when he will return, but we all know it won't be any soon."

Evelyn and Michael then moved on and explored more of the party. There was a cornucopia of delicious food on the table and cool nineties and eighties songs blaring out over the speakers, so the environment was very pleasant.

"Ugh, I'm glad there aren't any oysters here," Evelyn whispered to Michael, stepping up to her tiptoes to reach his ear. Michael laughed. A deep, rich laugh resonated in the air long after he was done laughing. It made Evelyn smile.

"I'm glad there isn't any alcohol either, since it is a children's party. But, the Lord knows how much you would have taken the liberty to drink," Michael teased her.

Evelyn tried to scowl, but her throat bubbled up with laughter. She bit her lips to stop it from spilling over, but Michael had already seen her suppressing her mirth, and his ocean blue eyes twinkled mischievously.

"Yes, I'm glad I haven't had anything to drink either. I totally forget everything after I get drunk," Evelyn said.

This was not true. In fact, Evelyn had the highest alcohol tolerance of anyone Michael knew. But she liked to pretend she had forgotten everything she had done in her inebriated state so that she would not have to face the consequences for them later on.

Michael knew that very well, but he still let Evelyn get away with it because he understood her need to run away from her problems, to hide them and try and drown them in a bottle. Little things like this were the reason why Evelyn was so sure Michael was her soulmate, and she was lucky she had married him.

Michael walked away to get them both one of the fruity juice drinks that were being served, and Evelyn wandered nearer to the pool, blankly looking at the waves in the water that splashed over every time someone dived into it.

"Hey," Christian called, half in the water and half out, waving his arms in Evelyn's direction. Evelyn turned away from where she was staring blankly and toward Christian with a smile.

THE NEIGHBORHOOD

"Hey, Chris! Everything okay?" she asked.

"Yup, everything is fine," Christian called out. "Watch me see how long I can hold my breath, though."

"Okay," Evelyn said and counted to three, upon which Christian took a deep breath and pulled his head under the water.

Evelyn started looking at her digital watch to track the time. Thirty seconds passed by, then one minute, then one minute and thirty seconds…

It was only when an entirety of two minutes had passed by that Evelyn began to panic severely.

"Is he okay?" she asked Charlie, Kenna's son, who was swimming on the further end of the pool. But Charlie was too far away to hear her. Evelyn looked around her, but nobody was paying attention to Christian. She had no other option.

She determinedly took off her shoes and jumped into the pool. She found Christian and pulled her head above the water. She waited a moment, but she could not feel his chest moving up or down.

He wasn't breathing. She moved her hand to his carotid artery to check his pulse, but before she could do so, Christian started coughing. When Evelyn looked clearly, she noticed that Christian was not coughing. He was laughing!

He had pranked her.

Evelyn sighed and shook her head.

"Kids," she sighed.

The adults had already gathered around the pool to see what had happened, and they all looked at Evelyn sympathetically but applauded her.

Michael stood at the edge of the pool, waiting to wrap Evelyn into his arms to warm her as soon as she got out. Instead, Kenna stood beside him with a towel.

She wrapped the shivering Evelyn in the towel and shooed Michael away, taking Evelyn inside so that she could take a hot shower.

Once Evelyn was done with her shower, she noticed that Kenna had laid out dry clothes for her to change into. She walked out into the living room to see Kenna and Michael waiting for her.

Kenna handed Evelyn a steaming mug of coffee, made her sit on the sofa, and set a bowl of warm soup in front of her so that she could ward off any cold she might have caught as she dived into the pool.

"I'm happy you tried saving Christian. He should not have done that. That was him being very immature, but he did not expect you to jump into a pool or care about him that much. You surprised us all, Evelyn, but it did show us that you're one of us. You're a good person," Kenna said with a short laugh.

Evelyn felt warmth rise up to her cheeks and settle into her heart. She was happy that they finally found good neighbors. She was glad that Christian had jumped into the pool because that was the only way she could have gotten to experience how kind her neighbors were. Besides, it was a good learning experience.

"Chris *is* very mischievous," Evelyn admitted.

"Chris?" Kenna asked in surprise. "He lets you call him Chris?"

Evelyn nodded with a soft smile, which made Kenna break out into a smile of her own, and said to Evelyn, "He must already be bonding with you then. None of us are allowed to call him Chris. I'm happy for you."

Evelyn felt as if her heart had doubled in size there and then, and she felt an insane amount of fondness toward the twins wash over her.

"I like them, too," she said.

Evelyn started thinking of hosting her own little party once their new place was fully settled and inviting the neighbors for tea. She was sure all of them would love to meet the dogs, her little Roxy and Zeus.

It was only later when Evelyn was back home and starting to settle back on the sofa to read her book, that she replayed the scene back in her head and realized that there had been something off about the whole scene.

She thought about how she had not felt Christian breathe and the way he had immediately broken pretense as soon as she tried checking his pulse. But what Christian did not know was that it had already been too late.

Evelyn had already located his carotid artery, but the funny thing was when her fingers had moved over it, she felt an absence of any heartbeat.

Christian's heart simply did not beat.

Chapter 11

He Asked Me Out

Evelyn tore open the white envelope with its fancy, rested seal on the front. The emblem was an insignia of her high school, so she did not quite know what to make of it till she pulled out the neatly folded paper within.

She unfolded the white parchment and started reading it aloud.

"Dear Evelyn," she recited. "You have been cordially invited to the 20-year reunion of…"

Evelyn trailed off, staring at the rest of the letter in part incredulity and part despair.

"Twenty years?" she said with a wince at the thought.

"Twenty years!?" she exclaimed again, her voice louder this time. "Holy-"

Evelyn stopped herself mid curse because she was trying to give up on her cursing and then looked away from the letter, calling out to Michael in the other room, "Mike! I'm getting *old!*"

"About time you realized it, honey!" Michael called back, walking to the entrance of their bedroom. Evelyn turned to face him and scowled at his smug grin.

"You…" she shook a finger in his direction but then, finding nothing to say, just ended with an "Ugh."

Michael grinned and drew closer to her.

"Don't worry, Eve. You don't look a day over thirty," he grinned down at her petite frame.

It was true. Evelyn had a shorter, slight frame that made her look slightly frail despite being very athletic during her high school and college years. Unlike most other women, her skin was unwrinkled and unblemished and had a slight rosy tinge. Her eyes, instead of dulling, seemed to only brighten with age.

Evelyn usually attributed her glowing skin to her healthy diet and exercise regimen, and Michael supposed part of it was true. Still, he also knew that Evelyn was one of those timeless beauties that seemed to simply exude a certain elegance, regardless of how old they were. That very elegance made Evelyn look younger than she truly was.

Dale, their mutual friend, sometimes joked about how Evelyn seemed to *'age like fine wine.'* But then the same went for Michael. He was already well into his forties, but he was still built.

THE NEIGHBORHOOD

He had not let himself go, exercised every week, and his hair was thicker than Evelyn's, so he wasn't one of those men with thinning hair and receding hairlines.

"So, your reunion," Michael mused. "Are you going to go?"

Evelyn smiled up at him, her green eyes lighting up, "Of course, I'm going to go. I have so many people to meet. You want to come with?"

"Hell yeah!" Michael cheered. "When is it?"

Evelyn scanned the paper once again, her manicured nails holding onto the parchment delicately to not leave any pressure marks on it.

"This Saturday," she said after a quick recheck.

Michael dropped his gaze, avoiding her eyes, and said, "Eve, I think I have to work overtime this Saturday. I'm sorry."

"Oh," Evelyn said, slightly disappointed but moving on from it. That was one of the only things they ever fought about, Michael's overtime work on Saturday. It was not a usual thing, but sometimes, every three or so months, right before a big project, Michael usually had to pull overtime shifts to get things done, especially since he was a senior manager.

There were times when Evelyn sometimes dropped by to

check on him, and she almost always found him covered in dust and cement, shouting instructions to crane drivers.

"That's fine," Evelyn told him.

And it truly was fine. Some part of Evelyn knew she did not want Michael to tag along to her school reunion. It was not because she was uncomfortable with Michael's presence or ashamed of him. It was just that she did not want her high school life to mix with her present life. She was light years away from who she used to be back in high school in her head.

She was always extremely well-known, always stood out, and for some reason, the spotlight was always on her. The only difference between high school Evelyn and the present Evelyn was that back then, she was new to the spotlight, and she felt uncomfortable under it, but now, she was used to it.

Michael left the room, mumbling something to Evelyn about how he would make dinner for the rest of the week to make up for not being able to go with her. Evelyn thought it was a sweet gesture.

She picked up one of the bottles of wine hidden inside a compartment of the cabinet. She called it her *'emergency supply.'* Unscrewing the cork, she deliberated, for a brief moment, on whether she should pour some into a glass. She eventually decided not to and took a swig of the cool Sangria straight from the bottle, wincing slightly as the sweet liquid burned her throat. She wondered if she should have gone for the Rosè, but then again, she needed something stronger.

She gazed at the red liquid swirling around in the clear bottle and recalled the memories of another day when the sun had been just as bright and red in the sky.

***

"Eve," Saleen whispered across the desk, but Evelyn was too busy staring out at the reddened sun to pay attention.

"Psst," Saleen tried again, but to no avail.

Eventually, though, a very annoyed Saleen balled up a piece of paper and threw it at Evelyn's head. Evelyn turned and looked around, a slight scowl on her lips. Then, she met Saleen's eyes, and her scowl intensified.

"What!?" she whisper-shouted at Saleen, her scowl turning into an annoyed pout.

It was supposed to be choir class, but the choir teacher was not able to show up, so the students were given a free block where they had to sit in the classroom and work silently on their own projects. Evelyn had nothing to do, so she had resigned to staring out at the window and daydreaming.

"Colson Banks has been staring at you for the past one and

a half hours," Saleen told Evelyn, her voice bordering on slight excitement.

Evelyn glanced at Colson to make sure it was true, and to her surprise, he was actually staring right at her. Evelyn quickly turned away, a slight blush rising to her cheeks. She slapped her cheeks slightly and determinedly fixed her eyes away from him, onto the glassy window and the view beyond it.

The light fell on one side of her face and circled her dark hair in a halo of light, making her look almost ethereal. It was no wonder that Colson was staring at her.

Colson Banks was one of the most sought-after boys in their high school. He was tall, with mesmerizing eyes and pianist hands that were kept neat. Of course, it helped that he could sing, play the piano, and he had an affinity toward the arts. Most people had bets riding on him, claiming that he would become the valedictorian.

Colson Banks and his twin, Cameron Banks, were known as the heartthrob twins, and out of the two, Colson was a triple threat. He was the perfect combo of good looks, intelligence, and an amazing personality.

Truth be told, Evelyn had a crush on him. While most girls were crushing on Cameron and his *'bad boy'* appearance, Evelyn resolved that she would never be like one of the girls falling all over themselves to sleep with him. She was the kind of mature teenager who went for the nicer guys. She knew Cameron was bad news and his humungous ego was enough to make her decide he was not worth the tears or the dates.

Evelyn glanced back only to see Colson still looking at her. He caught her eye and winked straight at her. Evelyn turned back to her window so fast she felt her neck crick. Her heart was beating insanely fast, and she could hear her pulse pounding in her ears.

"Be still, my heart," she said, quoting Shakespeare. But she was also serious about it. She could feel nerves filling up her veins, and a jittery feeling washed over her. She felt slightly giddy.

She shook her head slightly, annoyed at herself for letting her emotions control her. The bell rang, and Evelyn let out a sigh of relief.

"Finally," she muttered. "No more awkward staring matches with my crush."

She turned slightly and almost shrieked. Colson stood behind her, wearing an amused smile on his lips, already looking down at her.

"Hey Eve," Colson said, his eyes wrinkled in a slight smile. Evelyn had never before seen someone whose eyes smiled when they were happy. But Colson's somehow did.

"Hi, Colson!" Evelyn exclaimed, glad to hear that her voice came out steady. "Is there anything I can help you with?"

Colson looked slightly awkward and rubbed the back of his neck.

"I have a party at my house tonight at seven. Please come," he exclaimed.

Evelyn tried to disguise the look of surprise on her face and smiled brightly. She hitched her stylish purple knapsack higher on her shoulder determinedly and said, "Of course. Do you think I can bring along a friend?"

At this, Colson blushed. A reddish hue washed up his cheeks, and Evelyn marveled at the way he betrayed his shyness. She almost laughed because of how adorable he was.

Colson coughed awkwardly and said, "Uh… no. It'll just be us, so I don't want her to third wheel or feel out of place."

Evelyn choked on air.

"Oh…Uh…I thought it was going to be a party so it would have more people?"

Colson flinched slightly, smiled sheepishly, and said, "Yeah, actually, it's not a party. It will be just the two of us. I thought we could have dinner, catch a movie and maybe hang out in the park later and stargaze?"

"That sounds amazing. I'll be there," Evelyn said with a soft smile, shyly tucking back a strand of hair that fell in front of her eyes.

"It's okay," Colson said with a smile of his own. "I'll pick you up."

"Oooohh, ever the fancy gentleman!" Evelyn teased, losing part of her awkwardness.

"Yeah, well. I'm trying my best," Colson replied. Then he waited and then added as an afterthought. "I usually go out with my friends after a big match, but I wanted to do something special for a change. And that's you. Spending time with you would be special for me."

It was Evelyn who blushed this time. She hid her face behind the falling strands of her dark hair, and Colson laughed at her adorableness.

"So, I'll pick you up at seven after the match?" he asked.

"Seven it is," Evelyn confirmed and then watched as Colson nodded at her, winked, and started walking backward, keeping his eyes on her. It was only when he had to turn the corner that he finally tore his gaze from her and looked away.

"Well. That was cute!" Saleen squealed from behind Evelyn, making her jump slightly. Evelyn had still been gazing at Colson with a dazed expression on her face.

Evelyn shook her head and looked away.

"But the Banks twins are so hot," Saleen gushed, much to Evelyn's immense dismay. She did not mind Colson, but Cameron was an absolute playboy and someone she never wanted to be affiliated with. She had no idea why all the girls at school had a crush on him.

"Ugh, Saleen, stop!" Evelyn exclaimed and then changed the subject, starting to walk to her next class. "You gonna watch me cheer on Friday then?"

"Heck yeah!" Saleen cheered, dropping the subject. "I can't wait!"

"Yeah, I can't wait either," Evelyn said, with a soft, secret smile on her face.

***

Evelyn pulled herself back to the present and to the bottle of wine in her hand. She took a deep swig, swirling the sweet Sangria around in her mouth.

"I can't wait to see all hell break out when I show up there all badass," she said with a silent, knowing smirk. She was no longer the soft, naïve girl she was back then. Instead, she was a strong, elegant woman now, and she would watch love to watch them panic, trying to wrap their heads around how successful she had become.

Chapter 12

The Angel Kids

Christian and Bailey sat in the treehouse that they had built. They had a small park within walking distance of their house, so Bailey and Christian had decided to make it their regular haunt. They hung out around there whenever one of them wanted to be alone or just in silent company.

Bailey called it her 'safe space,' a place where she could feel calm, unjudged, and vent all her frustrations if need be. The park did not have a lot of frequent visitors since most children preferred the bigger park, the one with the football field, that was just opposite their school grounds. Even adults preferred the bigger park, so the twins had the smaller one all to themselves.

It had been Christian's idea to build the treehouse. He had taken permission from the relevant authorities, and he and Bailey had set to work building a massive, two-story construction. It was easier for them to do it because they had used their angel speed, super strength, and wings. Christian often joked about how they didn't need ladders because they had wings.

The treehouse was made entirely out of polished redwood, with impeccable carvings on the wooden panels, courtesy of Bailey. It had a rope ladder going up it, even though the twins wouldn't need to use that. The main purpose of the rope ladder had been to avoid any suspicion from humans. In addition, they had decorated it with soft, colorful rugs and flowy curtains that gave it a homely feeling. Bailey often felt that it was more of a home to her than the actual house she lived in.

Bailey was settled back on a cushioned bean bag, curled up with a book, and Christian was pacing back and forth across the space. His brow was furrowed in slight concentration as he thought.

"Oh, for Heaven's sake…Chris!" Bailey exclaimed all of a sudden. "Stop stomping on the floor like that. I'm trying to read here, and you're distracting me."

Christian frowned, and for a second, he looked so much like Evelyn that Bailey faltered. She sighed and closed her book, put it beside her, and then turned to Christian.

"Okay, tell me, what's up?" she asked.

Christian sat down beside Bailey with a thump, but his frown didn't ease up, even when he started to speak.

"Maybe we should tell her now?" he asked.

Bailey shook her head, her hair spilling over her shoulders and falling messily around her.

"Tell Evelyn she's our mom? What else, that we're her half-angel children who came back and are trying to protect her?" Bailey remarked with a smidgen of sarcasm in her tone.

Chris looked at her like he didn't think it was a bad idea.

"She's going to think we're insane, Chris!" she scolded him, her voice rising slightly.

Christian shrugged.

"Well, she needs to know! It's not like we can just keep this as a secret from her," he countered back calmly.

"Look, even if we do tell her, she probably won't believe us, Bailey tried to rationalize, gathering up her hair and piling it into her hands before using the scrunchie she had been wearing on her wrist to tie it up. "She will either think we're lying or crazy, or she might even feel like *she's* the one who's going crazy."

"I know. I know," Christian said in dejection. "But I really feel this weird urge to protect mom and Michael."

"Yeah, I know. I do, too," Bailey said with a deep sigh.

"I think she has started to guess already because of her empath skills. She probably senses an aura from us. And even without the aura, it's pretty suspicious. We have the same exact hair color and eye color as her, even though it's a rare combo, so I'm pretty sure she has already noticed that." Christian mused.

It was true. The twins both had beautiful brunette hair that curled ever so slightly at the bottom, making it look like they had gotten it styled that way. It was the same kind of effortless hairstyle that Evelyn had. In addition, their eyes were a bright, vivid green that sparkled like emeralds in the sunlight.

Having green eyes and thick, dark hair was uncommon where most people were generically blonde and blue-eyed. The twins looked almost exactly like younger versions of Evelyn. Both of them were pretty sure that Evelyn had noticed that. In fact, Evelyn actually had noticed the resemblance she shared with them, but she hadn't pointed it out because she thought she was just being silly.

Christian ran a hand through his dark hair wistfully.

"I miss my white hair," he commented. Once they had died and gone to heaven, their appearance had changed, and they had looked more like the rest of the angels. Full angels had bright silver hair, the palest skin, and shockingly purple eyes. All of them looked alike and could only be differed based on their features.

The twins were only half-angels, though, so their skin had not taken on the marble-like tint that the rest of the angels had.

Instead, they had a healthy tan, like their mother. However, they, too, had white hair and purple eyes when they were in heaven.

"I don't," Bailey spoke up automatically. "I like looking like this. This way, I look more like mom."

Her eyes softened when she thought about Evelyn. She loved her mother dearly, even though she was less expressive about it than Christian was. Christian was more of the temperamental, emotional kind. Even in heaven, he got into trouble all the time because of how mischievous he was.

Bailey, however, was more of the calm, rational type. She was the ideal type of daughter that every parent wanted. She was calm, understanding and she displayed a keen sense of empathy that surprised many adults. Of course, she had inherited that from her mother as well.

Christian picked up the book Bailey had been reading and started flicking through it. He put it back down with a grimace. He was not the biggest fan of reading. In fact, he usually did all he could to avoid reading. He, unlike Bailey, preferred pulling pranks.

The thought of the water incident that had terrified Evelyn made him smirk slightly. He felt awful because he had scared her, but it had been slightly funny too. And he never would have expected her to jump in the pool to save him. It made him realize that their earthly connection made her care about them despite the short time she had known them for. She did not know they were her children, but she could still somewhat sense it.

"The look on her face when she checked my pulse was so funny!" Christian said, his voice bordering on a slight laugh.

Bailey groaned in frustration.

"Don't even remind me of the water incident, Chris!" she exclaimed. "Evelyn was this close to figuring out there was something weird about us."

She held her finger and a thumb in a slight circle to emphasize how closely they had escaped suspicion.

Angels breathed too, but they did not require as much air, so their breathing was slower. Even their heartbeat was less rapid than the heartbeat of a human being. Angel's hearts beat once every two minutes. It was so that if a human accidentally discovered them, they would think that since they did not have a heartbeat, they were dead.

Christian suddenly winced, then shook his head and looked away.

"What?" Bailey asked him sharply, having caught his gesture.

"My wings are growing back. I can't keep them hidden anymore," Christian said.

Bailey nodded her head.

"Mine too. We are going to need to go visit heaven for a bit," she replied.

The twins could retract their wings, but it only lasted for two weeks. After that, they had to stretch their wings and fly for a bit, or else it would cause damage to their feathers. They could not really fly while they were on Earth since they did not want to be accidentally caught. The twins were both cautious. Sometimes Christian could be silly, but both of them were somewhat wise beyond their sixteen years of age.

"We are going to need to be more careful," Bailey said, furrowing her brow. "They have started getting closer to us now, and we have started interacting more. There are more chances for either mom or Michael to find out the truth."

Michael was the man who had married their mother, so he was their 'Earthly dad,' but neither of them was comfortable calling him 'dad' yet. Michael was not their biological father, but both, Christian and Bailey, liked him more than they had liked their actual father. Michael was warmer, kinder, and basically an overall better person. Christian, especially, was close to Michael.

"Yeah," Christian agreed. "Especially since mom is going to start having those vision dreams now."

Vision dreams were something the twins still did not fully understand. But apparently, since Evelyn had a strong empath aura, heaven had decided to send her these visons through her dreams to allow her to understand what was going on. It primarily allowed Evelyn to come to terms with the twins being half-angel, her old trauma, her PTSD, and the existence of the heavenly realm.

The higher-ups in heaven believed that it would be hard for humans to come to terms with all of their feelings of a sudden, regardless of how open-minded or empathetic they were. But surprisingly, they had found Evelyn very pliable since she did not need a lot of convincing. Moreover, she was more 'heavenly inclined' than most humans tended to be.

Bailey pinched the area between her eyebrows to relieve her stress.

"I have no idea how we are going to do this. There is no way we can introduce ourselves to mom, and even when we find a way, we will be too attached to leave them. I really, really just found my parents and I don't want to part from them so soon," she said.

Her eyes welled up with tears, and she tried not to let them fall. But she blinked her eyes, and a tear trailed down her cheek anyway. It dripped onto the wooden floor, and the area where it fell shifted and grew into a small sunflower.

THE NEIGHBORHOOD

Angel tears were golden, regardless of whether the angels were on Earth or in heaven. And when angel tears fell on the ground, sunflowers grew from them. That is why sunflower fields are, at once, the saddest but also the most beautiful places on Earth. Sad because that is where angels weep but also beautiful because their tears sprout into flowers that always turn toward the sunlight. They symbolize, to angels, the hope that stems from grief and closure.

Christian drew Bailey into a hug and patted the top of her head.

"It will be fine," he reassured her, his eyes on the sunflower.

Bailey shook her head in agreement, and Christian let her go. She wiped her tears with the palm of her hand, making sure no more tears fell to the floor, and smiled weakly. She stepped back to pick up her book and watched as Christian plucked the solitary sunflower and held it up to the sunlight.

Unlike most flowers, sunflowers that grow from the tears of an Angel are eternal. They never wither away, nor do they die when plucked. Christian looked away from the flower and smiled at Bailey.

"You want to go give this to mom?" he asked.

"Do you think she likes sunflowers?" Bailey asked back.

Her voice was stronger, and some of her spirits had returned.

"I have a feeling mom loves sunflowers as much as we do. And I think she will love this one even more if we give this to her," Christian said.

"But it will never die. Won't she find it odd if it doesn't wither away in a day or two?" Bailey wondered.

Christian sent Bailey a conspiratorial wink and said, "Well then, she can just consider this as a hint from us."

Bailey laughed at Christian's absurd ideas and nodded her head. The sunflower would be their secret hint. Giving the angel tear sunflower to their mother would be a silent symbol telling her to have hope. And hope was something all of them desperately needed.

Chapter 13

School Party

Flashback

Evelyn was jittery all over with nerves. It was finally the Friday she had been waiting for. The match was over, their school had won, and Colson was going to be at her house to pick her up for their date. She glared at her wardrobe and the racks of clothes that hung there.

"Why can't I just decide what to pick?" she whined.

She stared at the carved brown wood of the cupboard as if expecting it to pick her clothes out for her. There was already a pile of dresses strewn over the bed. She didn't want to wear black or red because they seemed too flashy for a party at Colson's house, but she didn't want to wear whites or greys either since they seemed too drab.

She finally settled on a blue, flowy summer dress with patterned lace at the edges. It made her look tall, despite her short frame, and emphasized her curves. She finished the look with some plain white converse instead of going for heels. The outfit made her look both cute and sexy at the same time. She hesitated over the mascara bottle but went for it anyway, applying some to her eyelashes and adding a slight dash of tinted gloss to her lips.

She looked beautiful.

Her cheeks were naturally flushed a light pink, making her look like she was at the peak of youth. Her green eyes were lit excitedly, and then she was fully aware of how breathtaking she looked. She was also extremely nervous because she did not know what to make of the party and Colson.

The bell rang, and she rushed to open the door. She assumed it was Colson, and she didn't want to keep him waiting. She opened the door to see Colson standing there with a single red rose in his hand.

Evelyn smiled and took it from him, tucking it behind her hair shyly. Colson was still staring at her, slightly open-mouthed and dazed. He blushed when he caught her looking at him strangely.

"Hey, Cole!" Evelyn chirped.

"Hey Eve," Colson said with a stutter. "You look beautiful. I'm blown away."

Evelyn just smiled in response.

"Thank you, Cole," she said, then looked him up and down

to see him dressed in a white shirt and some blue jeans.

"You look good, too," she complimented in turn.

They stood awkwardly at the door for a moment before Colson coughed.

"You ready to leave?" he asked.

"Yeah, sure!" Evelyn laughed slightly, giving him her arm and letting him escort her outside to his father's blue Audi. Everyone at the school was super loaded, but the Cameron and Colson twins came from an old-money family. Their father was connected with the mayor and had higher connections than the rest of them.

The car was quiet while they drove to Colson's house. Evelyn was expecting it to be comfortable silence, but it wasn't. It was not awkward, but Evelyn still deliberated, turning on the music because of how heavy the silence had become. When they reached the house, Evelyn balked at the number of cars parked outside the place. Colson parked and, noticing Evelyn's nervousness, grabbed her hand.

He held it gently for a moment, telling her with his eyes that she could do this.

"Don't be afraid," Colson said gently.

"I'm not," Evelyn clarified, shaking her head. "Just slightly hesitant."

Colson nodded, and they left the car, heading inside. The party was in full swing. High schoolers stood around with bottles of beer and red solo cups in their hands. It was wilder than Evelyn thought it would be and more crowded. There seemed to be no space to move, and it took Evelyn a while to learn to maneuver around the space.

The house was huge!

It had crystal chandeliers and bright halogen lights. Despite all the beer bottles on the counter, the kitchen was a state-of-the-art affair, equipped with the sleekest stove and cabinets. Evelyn gaped as she took it all in.

Colson laughed at her reaction.

"Do you like it?" he asked, fawning over her cuteness and wondering if she could get any more adorable.

Evelyn nodded, and Colson laughed again.

"She makes me happy," he said in a soft whisper as if the realization had just hit him. However, the din of the music was too loud, so Evelyn never heard the words.

He handed her a beer, and Evelyn drank half of it at once without pausing for breath. She was already very thirsty, and for some reason, she could not really taste it while she was drinking it.

It was only when she moved the bottle away from her mouth that she felt the bitterness of beer and the stinginess that went down her throat and made her wince slightly.

She looked up to see Colson gaping at her.

"Slow down, Eve!" he said, half in awe.

Evelyn looked at him with slight guilt, but she downed the rest of the bottle anyways. Colson shook his head fondly and handed her another one. He then took her on a tour of the house. She took in the house and its multiple rooms, storing it in her memory.

While he was showing her around, they bumped into quite a few classmates, and Colson stopped to say hi every time. It bothered her slightly because Colson had told her it would be quiet and more of a private thing. She did not think she would have to interact with so many people.

She did not like the way the boys were staring at her, either, and it did not seem like Colson was aware of how awkward she felt.

The last place Colson took her around was the pool. Evelyn enviously watched the teenagers having a blast in the warm pool water and turned to Colson with a slight pout.

"You didn't tell me it was going to be a pool party," she

complained girlishly.

Colson laughed and bopped her nose, making her smile.

"I asked Saleen to pack an extra swimsuit for you, don't worry," he told her.

He took her by the hand and to his room to give her the swimsuit. It was a two-piece green outfit, with lace at the edges, as if to match her dress. She changed into it and assessed herself in the mirror. It did not look bad on her, and she was glad she had not had too much beer to feel self-conscious about herself.

She left the room to see Colson, who politely kept his eyes on her face instead of letting them wander. He didn't pay attention to all the stares they were getting from the others as he led her to the pool, even though Evelyn felt every gaze acutely, and it made her feel like tiny insects were crawling all over the back of her neck.

Colson's eyes fell on the empty bottle in Evelyn's hand.

"Want me to get you another one?" he asked.

Evelyn nodded eagerly, already dipping toe foot into the pool water to check the temperature. She looked away and saw Colson had already left to get her drinks. She shrugged and lowered herself into the pool, relishing the way the water felt against her skin. She did not know how to swim, but she was fond of it, nonetheless.

She saw Colson wading toward her from across the pool, two bottles of beer in his hand. She furrowed her eyebrows because it had only been a second or so since Colson had left, and she wondered how he was back so soon. She knew for a fact that the kitchen was on the other side of the house.

"Do you like the house?" Colson asked, pulling her away from the crowd and into a more secluded part in the L-shaped pool.

Evelyn looked at him in confusion.

"Haven't you already asked me that?" she asked.

Colson furrowed his brow.

"I did?"

Evelyn nodded. She distinctly remembered him asking her that while they stood together in the kitchen. Then she shook her head and said, "I don't remember."

She realized that she was just probably tipsy, or maybe she had just imagined him asking.

She noticed that Colson was wearing an earring in his left ear, and she touched it slightly. She hadn't realized his ears were pierced. And she had no idea why she had not seen it when he had come to pick her up. She figured maybe he had worn it when he had gone to get her some drinks.

Colson was looking at her instead.

"You look hot, babe!" he said, letting his eyes drop to the curve of her shoulder since the rest of her was underwater.

"Babe?" Evelyn asked, feeling a blush rise to her cheeks. She was nervous suddenly, even though she had been alone with Colson before, and she had never felt nervous then. She liked his use of pet names. She had always loved pet names.

"Mhmm," Colson hummed and nodded. "You have no idea how hard it has been trying to look away from you," he said.

His voice was deep, and it flowed over Evelyn like melted chocolate. She shivered, and a flash of a smirk crossed Colson's lips. He pulled her closer to himself, and she let him, too mesmerized by his eyes to worry about anything else. She had just had two beers; she had no idea why she felt this was it when she was not even tipsy.

She looked back up to see Colson's eyes fixed on her lips. He lifted a hand and cupped her cheek with it, letting his thumb settle just below her eye. He moved it, slowly, till it rested over the bridge of her nose and then traced her lips.

Evelyn felt like she couldn't breathe. She couldn't think. All she could do was stare at Colson wide-eyed. And when he moved closer and kissed her, she couldn't even do that. Her eyes were open, but her vision felt hazy till she finally closed her eyes and moved her lips with his.

Colson broke away, but Evelyn followed him as if unwilling to stop. She kissed him this time, and he reciprocated.

Colson broke away and looked at her wide-eyed.

"Wow…I-" he sounded like he was at a loss for words. He looked away, avoiding Evelyn's eyes as if panicked.

"I gotta go," he told her and then said it again, in a more urgent voice. "I have to go."

He swam away from her, leaving her staring behind him.

A minute or two later, he was back while Evelyn was still in a daze. But she noticed something was off about him. He had seemed edgier before, more intense. She noticed he was not wearing the earring anymore, and she assumed he must have slipped it off again. He frowned when he saw her looking all flustered. He had a beer in his hand, which he handed to her.

"You alright?" he asked her.

Evelyn looked away, waiting for the butterflies to flutter again, wondering why she wasn't feeling the same way she felt a while ago.

"You wanna go home now?" he asked.

"I-" Evelyn said. She did not want to leave, not after that kiss.

Colson smiled at her.

"You can't go home. You're drunk, and you shouldn't drink and drive. So guess you're gonna have to stay the night," he said with a slight smirk.

But again, his smirk was different this time. Again, Evelyn wondered how he could change personalities so easily, as if by the flip of a switch.

"Was that your plan from the start?" Evelyn asked him, suspiciously narrowing her eyes.

"Maybe," Colson said, with a teasing lilt to his voice.

Evelyn followed him as he climbed out of the pool, holding her hand and taking her to his room. Evelyn waited for the nerves to come back when they were alone, but they did not. She did not understand why Colson could not make her feel like she did a while ago. She looked away and sat on his bed.

Colson pointed a thumb at the door.

"I'm gonna wait for the party out, clean up and sleep on the couch. You can get some sleep here," he said.

THE NEIGHBORHOOD

Evelyn wanted to protest, but she felt tired all of a sudden. She flopped down on the bed, her swimsuit already beginning to dry out because of the heat of the summer. Colson pulled the blanket over her and tucked her in. Then he walked out of the room, softly closing the door behind him. Evelyn stared at the door for a minute or two before a wave of sleep overtook her, and she fell asleep.

When Evelyn woke up again, it was to the feeling of hands on her face. Fingers were tracing the bridge of her nose and her lips, travelling down to her chin. She opened her eyes to see Colson above her.

But he seemed different.

He didn't seem like the soft Colson who had asked her to stay over. Instead, this seemed like the Colson who had kissed her in the pool. The earring in his ear was back. He smiled down at her when he saw her looking up at him with those huge, green eyes.

"You're awake?" he asked, his voice deeper and slightly hoarse.

Evelyn only nodded, slightly dazed by the sensation of his finger on her jaw. She felt warm and slightly feverish. But she knew she was not ill. She leaned her cheek into his hand.

Evelyn fixed her eyes on his earring, trying to keep her

breathing even.

"You're so beautiful," Colson groaned. "So fucking beautiful."

His eyes dipped lower, below her jaw, to the collar bone left exposed by the blanket that she had been covered in. His eyes darkened, their pupils dilating, and he closed them, his hands fisting up as if he was in pain.

"Fuck!" he muttered and moved his hand to her clavicle, letting it hover just above her cleavage.

"Can I touch you?" he asked. His voice was begging her, pleading with her. And she found herself unable to say no to him. She nodded.

He trembled over her before saying, "Your voice, baby girl. You need to say it. I need to hear you allow me to do this to you."

Evelyn flushed, and her body felt like a mesh of live wires.

"Yes," she said, her voice strong and decided. She wanted him.

That was all the consent be needed. He let his hand trace her collar bone, slowly moving his finger lower and lower while his other hand pulled the blanket away.

Evelyn moaned. She ached. She ached to have him fill her, to feel him inside her. She leaned up and kissed him.

He groaned into his kiss and let himself lay on top of her, making sure most of his weight onto his arms. He dragged kisses down her jaw, to her neck and lower, undoing her bra and then closing a hot mouth over her left nipple.

One hand hovered over her stomach, playing with the edge of her panties. Evelyn whimpered and thrust her hips upward involuntarily against his hand.

He was so slow, so deliciously, achingly slow, and she couldn't handle it. She felt as if she could orgasm, and he hadn't even touched her yet.

She felt his lips tilt up into a smirk against her nipple, and he bit her lightly. She gasped, and he looked up to see her flushed face.

"I like you below me," he said and, without waiting for her to reply, started laying small, open-mouthed kisses on her flat stomach. She jerked her hips against him, trying to get him to move. He stopped kissing her. The hand on the edge of her panties stopped playing with the lace. He moved away.

Evelyn felt cold air wash over her.

"No. No," she said, unable to mutter anything else.

"Have you ever done this before?" he asked her.

Evelyn shook her head, saying no.

"You're sure you want to do this with me. I'll be gentle. Let me worship your body. Can I?" he asked.

Evelyn nodded, then she caught his gaze, and, understanding he needed a verbal response, she uttered a "Yes."

That was all the approval he needed, Colson proceeded to ravish her thoroughly, and once they were done, she fell asleep in his arms.

She was still in Colson's arms when she woke up, except he was awake and looking down at her. She furrowed her brow when she took in his smile; it looked different from last night, gentler but also unfamiliar.

He did not seem like the same person. She stared at his smile till his face blurred from view, and then she noticed something else. His earring was gone. She did not understand. She felt as if he had somehow developed bipolar disorder.

"Good morning, Eve!" Colson chirped.

"Going from saying babe to Eve again?" Evelyn joked.

"Huh?" Colson said, his brow slightly furrowed, "I never called you babe."

Evelyn laughed, "Okay."

She winked at him as if to assure him that they were not

going to talk about last night if he did not want to, but it just made him more confused.

"My twin made pancakes. Want some?" Colson asked.

"Your twin?" Evelyn mused, "Oh! Cameron!"

She shook her head no.

"Want me to drop you home?" Colson asked, waiting for her to say something more.

"Ah, yes, please," Evelyn said, making a move to get off and then realizing her clothes were scattered around the place. She could ask Colson to get them, but she felt slightly shy about the whole ordeal, so she just blushed and asked him for space so that she could get dressed.

For some reason, she felt that something was wrong. Colson did not seem like the person she had slept with, and he seemed unaware of everything. The only thing Evelyn felt, even as she reached home, was a sense of confusion and deep regret.

Chapter 14

Home Sweet Home

Holly and garland decorated the windows on the street. A layer of snow had settled on the road, but the air was just deliciously chilly instead of freezing cold. Evelyn suspected the lack of bitter cold had something to do with the heating system and the glass dome that covered the entire neighborhood, but she did not ask.

Sometimes asking about things took the magic out of them. Each street had its very own Christmas tree at the end, fully decorated with homemade baubles and topped off with the most brilliant of stars. The entire neighborhood looked like something out of Norman Rockwell's work.

Evelyn drew aside her maroon curtain and peered outside, her lips tilting into a girlish smile as she looked at the decorations.

"God, I love this time of the year," she said happily, letting the curtain fall and looking at Michael. He was setting dinner plates and candles on the table, putting the finishing touches to the dinner party they were planning on having. He hummed in response to her excitement.

"What time are we going to go pick up your parents?" Michael asked. He was painfully meticulous about everything in his life. Always detail-oriented to a tee. And there were times when it irritated the hell out of Evelyn, but she had learned to cope with it. In many ways, she was the beginning, and Michael was her continuation. She was the pianist, and Michael was the music sheet she needed to guide her.

He was the one who complimented her perfectly. She was messy, and he was tidy. She was short, and he was tall. They were like the perfect fit in a jigsaw puzzle, but that did not mean that they never disliked anything about each other.

"Well, what time do they get in again?" Evelyn asked Michael.

"5:30," he informed her, sighing slightly at how clueless she was about everything. "They land at Portland International Jetport."

"We need to figure out an amazing dinner menu," Evelyn mused slightly.

"Yes, absolutely, I agree! Should we have the chef whip something up?" Michael asked.

"Yeah. That would definitely make it easier on us. I'll give the chef a call to confirm," Evelyn said with a slight smile, turning a page of her book.

"No. I'll do it, Eve; you relax and drink your eggnog," Michael quickly interjected, not wanting her to be bothered. He knew she liked holiday seasons, and Christmas was her favorite, so he wanted her to be able to enjoy it to the fullest.

Evelyn winced little when she heard him say eggnog. Not because it was not eggnog, it was just that she had slipped a little whiskey into it, so she was already slightly tipsy. However, she chose not to divulge that little bit of information to Michael since she knew he would probably disapprove of it. But she really did need to be hammered before she could deal with her family.

It was not that they were bad, per se. It was just that they could be slightly…intense.

Her side of the family was amazing, but she had to admit that they were all tended to be slightly berserk, especially at this time of year. First, they drank and sang Christmas carols while her father played the guitar. And then they usually had a game night, which was where everything went downhill.

Unfortunately, game nights almost always ended in fistfights since they were very competitive. She was looking forward to it, but at the same time, she was not. Being an empath meant all of her senses were already heightened, so dealing with all of her family together and their heightened excitement tended to be harder on her.

***

Evelyn and Michael reached the airport early and watched as all the planes landed, waiting for their families to arrive. Something about the airport always calmed Evelyn, which was out of the ordinary, especially because she usually wasn't a fan of large crowds. Michael bought both of them some warm pretzels. Evelyn did not think they were a good substitute for the chef's bread rolls, but she figured they would do.

"Eve, calm down! Stop biting your nails," Michael chided her, pulling her hand away from her mouth and holding it in his own hands. He winced slightly because of how cold they were, but he did not complain.

"I'm calm. I just really want everything to be perfect! There is just never enough time. I want them to like this neighborhood, and I really want them to approve. I don't really care about other people's opinions, but these are my parents, and I just-" Evelyn trailed off, her voice falling flat as if her frustration could no longer be expressed in mere words.

"Eve, Eve, Eve! Remember what your therapist says?" Michael asked in a calm voice, wrapping an arm around her shoulders and trying to calm her down. "Count to ten. Breathe!

Worry is going to kill you."

"Mike. Shut it. Eat your damn pretzel," Evelyn said with a slight temper, but her worry was somewhat forgotten. It made her smile. She liked how Michael knew exactly what to say to calm her down. Michael laughed in response, not minding her quip, and brushed his hair out of his face, making his eyes look even more brilliant.

"We need to cut your hair too, honey. It's getting wild," Evelyn said.

"Yeah, yeah, your sister can do that," Michael said, waving off her concerns.

Evelyn's sister owned a salon. But Evelyn had been trying to convince her to build one in their neighborhood. That would be way more cost-efficient and newer. Also, Evelyn just wanted all her family with her.

***

At 5:30, they headed to the terminal to find their family. They were the last ones out of the plane, and all of them were arguing, but then they saw Michael and Evelyn.

"Hi Eve!" Evelyn's father called out, waving at his daughter. He hugged Evelyn upon reaching her, then turned to Michael and shook his hand.

THE NEIGHBORHOOD

"Girls!" Evelyn screamed and squeezed her sister and nieces into a giant hug. "We missed you all so much!" she gushed.

"Mom and Karen!" she said and pulled them into a hug before stepping back. "I'm so glad you are all here!"

"Ok, we had a company van drive us here, so we will call them to get us now," Michael informed the family.

The van turned out to be waiting for them. So they all piled in and off to the neighborhood they went. When they arrived at Evelyn's house, the expression on her family's faces answered all the anxieties she had. She realized she truly had nothing to worry about.

"Wow, aunt Eve this is awesome!" Diana, one of the kids, screamed.

"Oh my God! It's so beautiful here!" Evelyn's sister, Rosa, gushed. They pulled up to Bliss, and their driver got all the luggage and brought it over to the house.

"Make yourselves at home, and dinner will be ready soon! Chef prepared us lobster bisque with rolls and filet mignon for dad and Michael, of course!" Evelyn chirped and sent a wink her father's way. She knew how much he liked filet mignon. It was what her father and Michael had initially bonded over during the initial stages of her relationship.

"I'm so happy you're all here!" Michael came into the room from the kitchen and handed Evelyn's father his favorite beer.

"That's my favorite son-in-law!" Evelyn's father cheered and patted him on the back.

"You say that to all of them, dad!" Rosa laughed.

"Yeah, but this one here really is good," Evelyn's father justified and laughed heartily.

Evelyn wished everyone was there. Unfortunately, her other sisters and brothers were off with their in-laws.

"Well, what do you say we go into town and get a real tree, Evie?" Evelyn's father said.

"Dad! We are fine with the fake ones this year. Besides, the kids will eat the needles and pee on a real tree," Evelyn told him, referring to Roxy and Zeus.

"Where are those little shits anyways?" Her father asked her.

"Oh, the neighbors' kids are babysitting them until we pick them up. I better go get them," Evelyn told him.

Evelyn walked to Tranquility, the house next to theirs, and rang the bell.

THE NEIGHBORHOOD

"Hi, Eve, the door is open!" Dora called.

All the doorbells had cameras. It was way better technology than the ring or anything like that and comparatively safer.

"Hey Dora, I'm here for the kids," Evelyn quipped. "How did they do?"

"Bailey! Christian! Come out, your-" Dora started to say and then stopped, looking horrified at her slip up. Evelyn narrowed her eyes, but Dora looked away.

"I mean, Eve is here. Oh, I'm getting old!" Dora said, covering her slip up and waving Evelyn over to the couch. Thirty seconds later, Roxy and Zeus came running at full speed, excited to see Evelyn. Christian and Bailey followed right behind the dogs.

"Hi Eve!" Bailey chirped. "They were so good today." She scratched Roxy behind the ear.

"Aww, I'm so glad to hear that!" Evelyn cooed. "Did you all have dinner? I had the chef prepare way too much food for the family that is over. Would you like to join us?"

The children smiled brightly, and it made Evelyn's heart feel warm.

"Yes! Yes! Can we, Dora?" Christian asked, turning pleading eyes to the babysitter.

"Well, miss Dora has to come along too! She can't sit here alone while we celebrate. So Dora, come join us!" Evelyn invited.

"Well, that sounds wonderful, dear. So, you go on ahead, and I'll be there soon after," Dora said.

"Okay, are you sure?" Evelyn asked hesitantly.

"Yes, I've got to run to Rangers Mall, anyways, but I won't be long," Dora explained.

"Okay then. We'll see you soon," Evelyn said, herding the kids out the door and across the street. "Come on, Roxy, Zeus, tell me all about your day."

Christian took the cue, narrating to Evelyn about how they brought the dogs to the dog park and made new friends.

"Oh, that's sweet," Evelyn said once he was done.

"What kind of friends?" she asked them to keep the conversation flowing.

"Well, they are-" Christian started to say, but Bailey elbowed him to make him stop.

"They were lab puppies," Christian finished and gave Bailey a mean stare, letting her know telepathically through their link, that that he had it under control and he was not going to slip up.

"Oh, I love puppies," Evelyn squealed. "Did you get

THE NEIGHBORHOOD

pictures?"

Just then, a thought clicked through Evelyn's mind, like a piece of puzzle fitting into the rest of the jigsaw. She realized there were no pictures in the kid's house, not even one of them as babies or school pictures.

'Bizarre,' Evelyn said to herself, making sure the children did not hear.

She decided to ask Dora about this later, but she put the thought of it out of her head as they finally reached her house.

"Hey everyone," Evelyn said, opening the door and letting everyone troop in. "I want you to meet some of the best neighbors in the world. This is Christian and Bailey. They babysat the granddogs today, so I invited them to eat with us and exchange gifts."

"Hi, kids!" Evelyn's father said, and Evelyn noticed the look on his face. She wondered if he, too, had seen the resemblance between her and the children. Evelyn shook the thought away and started to pass out presents.

"Let's do presents first," she said.

Dora came into the room.

"Hi everyone, I'm Dora," she introduced herself and sat down by the fireplace as directed by Evelyn.

"Eve, I have a special present for you. But you can't wear it until Christmas night," Dora said, handing her a jewelry box.

"Okay," Evelyn promised. She opened the box and saw the most amazing amulet she had ever laid her eyes on.

"Oh my gosh, Dora! This is too much!" Evelyn exclaimed. The necklace had golden wings that were inlaid with tiny diamonds along the front of it.

"Open it," Dora instructed with a gentle smile.

Evelyn obeyed and saw it had two different but also the most beautiful baby pictures inside the built-in frame.

"Oh, Dora, this is beautiful," Evelyn said. "Who are the babies?"

Even though she had asked, she instinctively already knew somehow. She suddenly remembered a dream she had once had with the exact same necklace.

"It's the twins," Dora told her. "It belongs to their mother. I want you to have it. You see, you are the most amazing person in their lives, and I don't know how to say this, but their father, well, he's not coming back. He passed on. He got very sick and didn't make it."

Evelyn gasped, surprised to hear the news of their sudden loss.

THE NEIGHBORHOOD

"Eve, I'm sorry to tell you this so close to the holiday, but his dying wish was for the kids to have a real family," Dora continued.

Evelyn's mouth dropped open in shock.

"Well, Michael did tell me if we ever adopted kids, he would want them to be older and out of the toddler stage," Evelyn tried stating lightheartedly to avoid the weight of the situation and come to terms with the news that she had just been handed.

"My heart is broken about the kid's dad. Do they know yet?" Evelyn asked Dora.

"No, sweetheart! I couldn't bear to tell them this close to Christmas. So please keep it between us for now," Dora said, her eyes downcast, and suddenly, she looked drained.

"You have my word," Evelyn said. She pulled Dora into a warm, consoling hug and noticed how cold the older woman was.

"Oh, Dora, let's get you back to the fireplace and get you a warm drink," Evelyn said, leading her back toward the inside of the room. Evelyn was shaking with all sorts of emotions.

Michael noticed her unease and pulled closer to her. "Honey, are you okay?" he asked gently.

"Yes, love, we'll talk later," Evelyn said, giving him a certain look that let him know she was serious about this.

Chapter 15

Finding Out

Evelyn felt sick as if something was churning in her stomach - a feeling of extreme discomfort. She crossed her arms over her body and shuddered slightly in the cold. Colson walked up being her and wrapped an arm around her shoulders.

"You okay, babe?" he asked gently. It was two weeks after the party. Colson and Evelyn had officially started dating. They were taking it slow, something Evelyn did not understand because they had already slept together on the night of the party. She thought Colson would be more physically affectionate with her after that, but he wasn't.

"Ah, I don't know," she said. "I just have a severe stomach ache. I don't know why. I think I've gained some weight lately."

Colson laughed.

"It must have been Rosa's cooking. The next time you come over, I'll ask her to make you something light," he said.

Evelyn hummed in agreement. Rosa was Colson's family chef. Evelyn loved her food, especially since most of Rosa's dishes were vegan and healthy but still managed to be extremely delicious. But she had to admit; she had been eating more.

Her appetite had increased drastically for some reason. She did not worry about it, though, attributing the increased hunger to stress and school work. Colson moved his hand under hers and started rubbing soothing circles on her stomach. Evelyn leaned back against him. He kissed her neck. Then her mouth.

The kiss grew more passionate till Colson started tugging on her shirt in an attempt to get it off. Evelyn broke the kiss.

"No, Cole," she told him, her voice firm.

"Wow. Shut down again. Nice way to make me feel like a man, babe," Colson said, his tongue dripping with sarcasm and a hint of bitterness. His mouth had curled up into half a scowl. Evelyn automatically felt slightly guilty for saying no, even though she shouldn't have.

"I'm sorry, babe. It's just that… I don't feel well today," she said.

Colson's scowl, however, did not ease up.

"Well, okay," he said, picking her bag up off of the floor. "C'mon, I'll take you home."

They drove over to Evelyn's house in Colson's newest Audi. It was a bright blue, and Evelyn thought it matched his personality well.

"Your house is nice," Colson told her, taking in the mismatched couches and embroidered pillows that made it look more homely. Personally, Evelyn liked the homey, woodsy touch that her house had, but one look at Colson told her he didn't particularly like it much. He was lying. Evelyn forced a smile. She gestured for him to put her bag down, which he did.

"Can I see your room?" Colson asked.

Evelyn blushed. She had mixed feelings. She had never had a boy be in her room before, but at the same time, she thought that they had already slept together and figured that it should not be as awkward.

But she did feel awkward around Colson. She was looking forward to the dangerous side he had shown her in the pool and when they slept together. But she never saw it. She did not remember seeing the earring again, either. In fact, she had never seen Colson wearing any sort of jewelry.

"Yeah," Evelyn said, making sure her voice was light and nonchalant. "Yup. This is the way to my room."

She guided him to her room and allowed him inside, extending her arms with a flourish. But Colson barely glanced around the room. He was looking at her. He closed the door behind himself and started walking toward her, backing her up till the back of her knees hit her bedstand.

He kissed her and pushed her onto the mattress, still not breaking the kiss. His hands slithered up under her shirt and palmed one of her breasts. Evelyn tried to get into it, but he simply did not seem to be affecting her. She fixed her eyes on his ear.

No earring.

There were no tingles, no pressure building up in the lower part of her stomach to signify an orgasm. It was not like last time.

But she wanted it to be.

It was that want that allowed her to let Colson touch her. That was why she allowed him inside her. When he was done, he lay on top of her, still pumping gently into her, but she felt nothing. She had not felt any sparks. There was no build-up and no orgasm.

He was inside her, but he did not feel as big as he had the last time, and she wondered what was different this time. Even his eyes had been different. The last time had been intense; he had kept asking for permission. This time he had barely looked her in the eyes or asked if she was okay.

He hadn't whispered in her ear, telling her all the things he was going to do to her before he did them. He had not loosened her up, feeling her to see if she was ready enough for him to fill her.

Last time, he had worshipped her body like it was a temple before he had ravaged it, completely ruining her for all other men.

But perhaps he had ruined her for himself, too, because this time, it felt fumbling and awkward. When he finally pulled out from inside her, she did not feel empty like she had before.

She felt…unfulfilled.

"Was it good, babe?" he asked, kissing her forehead.

Evelyn just nodded, not the least bit worn out or satisfied.

"I didn't expect our first time to be like this," Colson continued, not reading the mood. Evelyn really did not want to talk about it.

"First time?" she asked, with a slight scoff. "Yeah, right, babe. Stop joking."

"Want to go for round two?" she asked, hoping he would say yes. She wanted to know if another round would ignite the same feelings in her that it had previously.

Colson scoffed.

"Yeah, right, babe," he said, gesturing in the general direction of his lower body. "Give me time to recover first."

Evelyn frowned. The last time they had slept together, he had made her orgasm thrice and tired her out to the extreme but still had energy for more. He had shot her a wicked smirk each time she lost her control, as if seeing her in the throes of pleasure was more gratifying to him than his own orgasm. She wondered what had changed.

Colson got up and started collecting his clothes.

"I gotta go, babe," he told her. His phone pinged with a notification. He picked it up and briefly glanced at it. Then he sat back down on her bed, barely sparing her a glance.

"This was fun. Let's do it again, soon," he told her. He finished slipping on his shoes and looked at her still sprawled on the bed. He smiled, kissed her forehead, and then left.

He had made Evelyn feel slightly humiliated. She remembered how the last time they had done it, he had cuddled her close and told her she had done well, and he was proud of her for being so brave through it. He had thanked her for allowing him to sleep with her, made her feel valued. This Colson felt drastically different from that Colson.

She hated it.

***

Two weeks passed by in a blur.

Friday came, and Evelyn felt as if she was forgetting something. She thought about it until it hit her…her period was late. Evelyn was extremely healthy. She had never missed a cycle before, so she was really worried about being late. She fumbled with her phone, called her best friend, and waited, with bated breath, till she picked up her call.

"Hello?" a voice called down the line.

"Hey. Saleen! Oh my God, Saleen!" Evelyn said, her panic creeping into her voice. "Get here now," she whisper-shouted over the phone.

When Saleen reached Evelyn's house, Evelyn was curled up in a ball on her bed, holding her still-flat stomach.

"What's up?" Saleen asked, her voice concerned,

"My period is late," Evelyn said, lifting a tear-streaked face to look at her best friend.

"You hussy," Saleen said with a gasp. "I knew you probably slept with him. I mean, look at him. I don't blame you, girl."

Evelyn scowled, clearing away her tears, getting back some of her fire. Saleen grinned in response. She knew her words would automatically make Evelyn angry enough that she would forget her anger. There was a reason they were best friends.

"But it's okay," Saleen said, her voice serious and comforting, the mirth disappearing from it. "Let's not get ahead of ourselves and take a test first. I'll go drive you there."

Evelyn and Saleen drove to the pharmacy, bought the test, ignoring the judgmental looks they got and drove back home. Evelyn took the test and waited anxiously for the result, biting her nails. She was still trying to get rid of her habit of biting her nails when she was stressed.

Evelyn went to check on the test and felt her blood go still. It showed two red vertical lines. Positive.

"Oh shit. Oh, shit, oh shit!" Evelyn swore. "I'm pregnant!"

"It's okay. It's fine. We'll figure it out," Saleen said reassuringly, drawing a panicked Evelyn into her embrace and rubbing a soothing hand on her back.

"What will I do?" Evelyn asked tearfully.

"Look. Take this step by step. First, call Colson and tell him about it," Saleen instructed her calmly.

Evelyn did as she said, and they agreed to meet immediately.

She met him in the driveway while Saleen waited for her upstairs.

Colson walked up to Evelyn, a worried expression taking over his face.

"Everything okay?" he asked, pulling a teary Evelyn into a

hug. "You sounded off over the phone, and I get here to see you crying."

Evelyn shook her head, strands of dark hair flying around everywhere.

"No. I'm-" Evelyn paused, mid-sentence. "We're pregnant."

"What?" Colson exclaimed, pulling away from her as if her skin burned him. He completely moved, taking two steps away from her.

"How did you find out this soon? How is this possible?"

"This soon?" Evelyn asked, aghast. "Cole, pregnancy results show up at four weeks pregnant. My period was supposed to be two weeks ago. So that means I was already pregnant when we last slept together?"

"You were pregnant when we slept together?" Colson asked, looking disgusted. "You were cheating on me?"

"What do you mean? You know I was a virgin when I slept with you. I have only ever been with you!" Evelyn shouted at him.

"Then what do you mean you have been pregnant for four weeks. I slept with you two weeks ago?" Colson asked, confused but still angry.

"No, you didn't," Evelyn said, her brows furrowing. "We

slept together on the day of the party, remember? When you came to me in the pool."

She touched her left ear.

"You were wearing this dangling earring in your left ear, remember?" she said in an effort to jog his memory.

Colson flinched, and the confusion on his face turned to realization.

"Son of a bitch!" he said, turning and punching the hood of his car.

Evelyn moved closer to him, focusing on his ear. It wasn't pierced. Her heart sank.

"Cameron!" Colson growled. "You slept with Cameron. He's done this before, but I didn't think, I-"

Evelyn stepped closer to Colson, but he backed away from her, terrified. He fisted his hair in his hands, pulling at them in desperation.

"Cole!" Evelyn said, her tears falling, flowing down her cheeks, her heart twisted in worry and fear, not only for herself but also for her child.

"Hold me, Cole," Evelyn pleaded. "Tell me everything will be okay."

Her tears slid down her cheeks and fell on the pavement. Colson looked at her once, his own blue eyes looking utterly horrified. He looked away.

"I can't do this right now," he said. "I can't even look at you right now. Fucking hell. I'll go kill him."

"Please hold me, Cole!" Evelyn said, one last time, her voice breaking.

But he didn't look at her. He was too disgusted, too horrified.

"No," he told her.

A simple two-lettered and one-syllable word. He got into his car and drove off.

Evelyn lost the strength in her legs and fell to her knees in the driveway, looking at the leaving car. Her heart had broken when he had said "no," and it shattered around her as he drove away.

She did not want to live anymore.

Chapter 16

Confronting Cameron

Evelyn got a call from an unsaved number somewhere around 11:00 in the morning, just before her Mathematics AP class.

"Hello?" she asked, her tone hesitant.

"Hey, baby girl!" a deep voice called down the line. Evelyn's brows furrowed, and then her eyes widened in realization.

Cameron.

She wondered how she had not noticed before. The mannerisms, the tone, the pet names, everything about Cameron was so different from Colson. She wanted to hit herself for being so blind. But to be fair, she had not been completely sober on the night that she had slept with him.

"What?" Evelyn snapped down the phone. She was really mad at him, and she was not in the mood to take any of his excuses.

"I need to talk to yo-" Cameron started to say, but Evelyn cut him off.

"Talk to me?" Evelyn screeched, her voice rising. A few students turned to look at her but then looked away when they saw her glare.

"Ah, no, you little…fucker," she hissed in a slightly lower voice. "You don't get to talk to me after what you did to your brother and me! What is wrong with you two? How the hell could you just-"

Suddenly a huge hand grabbed Evelyn's wrist, enveloping it completely and pulling her across the hall and into the gym. Evelyn's eyes widened when she looked at whoever had pulled her. Then she narrowed her eyes and glared. Finally, she moved the phone that was still held to her ear and cut the call.

"What do you want, Cameron?" she snapped, peering at him under the hood that covered his face.

Cameron did not say anything. Instead, he simply pulled her into the weight room reserved for the athletes. Both of them knew that nobody would come into the weight room. It was a small space, only used to keep weights used by the basketball team, and since it was the off-game season, nobody would need them.

Evelyn pushed herself back against the wall and crossed her arms over her chest, glaring at Cameron.

"Look," Cameron started. "Let me explain-"

THE NEIGHBORHOOD

Evelyn huffed, interrupting him. "Let you explain? Are you listening to yourself right now? You slept with me, without my permissi-"

Cameron cut her off.

"I thought you knew," he said with a slight growl before he sighed and curbed his anger. His voice was softer when he spoke again. "I thought you knew it was me. I had no idea you would think it was Cole. We are so different. How could you not tell?"

Evelyn's eyes softened, and her face fell into contemplation. "The one in the pool. That was you?"

"Yeah," Cameron said, nodding emphatically.

"The one who slept with me that night of the party. You thought I knew it was you?" Evelyn asked.

Cameron nodded again, and as he did so, his hood fell off his head, letting Evelyn look into his beautiful green eyes. They did not hold any deceit, nothing to tell Evelyn that he was lying to her about this.

"I thought I had set up the mood while we were in the pool. You weren't even in Colson's room. You were sleeping in my room. The fucker probably thought it would be better to have me sleep on the couch while he slept in his own bed."

Cameron shook his head in slight disgust at his brother, a

scowl marring his features.

It was only then that Evelyn looked at him, really looked at him. He wore a black, baggy hoody and dark jeans with combat boots. He had a dangling cross earring in one ear and his favorite black one in the other. It was the same one he had been wearing the night they had slept together.

Just thinking about it made slight tingles rise in Evelyn's stomach, despite her not wanting them to. She let her eyes trace Cameron's figure, noting how he was slightly taller and slightly broader than Colson, more built because of all the working out he did.

She let her eyes trace his eyebrows, thick and a slight shade darker than his brother's. His nose was straighter, and his mouth was fuller, almost prettier than a girl's. And his eyes; his eyes were the most prominent difference, despite all the other differences being minor. His eyes were a deep blue, threaded with greens and greys, forming the waves on a sea of blue that his eyes seemed to be.

She remembered that Colson's eyes weren't as dark or as intense. Instead, Colson's eyes had been a plain blue, more bordering on grey than sapphire. However, Cameron's eyes were the most beautifully expressive pair of eyes she had ever seen.

"I thought you knew," Cameron repeated again, sounding

as if he was in immense pain. "That night, I asked you so many times if you were ready. Even before I knew you were a virgin, I asked you if you wanted to sleep with me. You said yes. Every time. And it sucks to find out that you thought it was some other man the entire time."

Evelyn's eyes softened. "But why would you try and make moves on me when you knew I was dating your brother?"

"I told him to stay away from you and that I had already set my eyes on you. It made him want to know what was so special about you, so he tried to invite you out to sleep with you. Wasn't it obvious?" Cameron asked, and suddenly, all the jigsaw puzzles fell into place.

Evelyn understood why Colson was so touchy, why he insisted on having sex, and why he was always so pushy about sleeping together.

"So you...But you're dating someone else, aren't you? That red-haired girl, Pearl?" Evelyn asked, her lips starting to form a scowl. "So you're just playing the both of us to try and live up to your playboy image?"

Cameron shook his head, looking extremely hurt at the accusation.

"Look. I would never do that. Yes, I sleep around, but the

women I sleep around with know it's a no-strings-attached thing. We're both consenting adults who have already decided things beforehand. And about my girlfriend," Cameron rolled his eyes. "Her name is Opal, and we broke up two months before we slept together. I broke up with her the first time I saw you."

"The first time you saw me?" Evelyn asked, curious.

"Mhmm," Cameron hummed. "The first time I saw you, you were singing along to this karaoke song in the bar. God, Evelyn, you have no idea how beautiful you were. Dark hair falling around you, making you look like a fallen angel, and those green eyes of yours seemed to shine right across the room and pierce my heart. You have no idea. Your voice, Evelyn! Your voice had me hooked. And all I wanted to do back then was to hold you and kiss you. I didn't even want to sleep with you. I just wanted to hold you and let your scent comfort me. You have no idea what you did to me," Cameron finished.

Evelyn's breath caught in her throat when she met his intense gaze. He looked at her with so much desire, with so much pain that she wanted to look away but, at the same time, was compelled to keep looking. It was just a want, a need, a desire. He looked at her with wonder, like a parched man in a desert, as if she was his only salvation.

She lifted a hand to his cheek and ran her palm across the

slight stubble on his skin. He closed his eyes as if in agony and allowed himself to rest his forehead against Evelyn's. Her heart flipped inside her chest, and for a second, she forgot how to breathe. She lifted herself on her tiptoes, slanted her head, and connected her lips with his.

She didn't move. He didn't either. They just stood there, unmoving, their lips meeting each other in the purest of kisses. It was more intimate than sex. The air around them was charged with electricity, and both of them could feel it right to the ends of their toes.

Evelyn did not know if she broke the kiss or him, but suddenly, they were no longer kisses. Instead, they were looking at each other with the most intense gaze, one that echoed with words that neither of them would ever say out loud. Then he smiled. And Evelyn felt as if her heart could burst.

He was beautiful.

She smiled back.

And they watched each other for what seemed an eternity but still felt too short.

"You got a nose piercing?" Evelyn asked, looking at him.

Cameron laughed huskily, a whisper of a laugh.

"Yeah. I guess I felt the need to inflict some extra pain on myself," he joked.

Evelyn hummed, smiling contentedly. Cameron made her feel something Colson never could. Just standing with him there, in that dusty weight room, proved to her that he somehow mattered more to her than Colson ever had.

"You wanna get out of here?" Cameron asked.

"Here? Where do you want to go?" Evelyn asked.

"Let me take you to the mall," he said.

"To the mall?" Evelyn asked. "Are we going to buy baby clothes?"

"Baby clothes?" Cameron wondered, tilting his head to the side and looking at her. "Why would you need baby clothes?"

Evelyn's heart sank. He didn't know.

She hesitantly held his hand and moved it to her stomach.

"When we slept together," she whispered shakily, even though there was no reason to keep her voice down. "Neither of us used protection and-"

She broke off and looked down at her hand, holding his to her stomach. "You're just a dad now. I understand if you don't want to take responsibility I-"

Cameron kissed her.

He kissed her so hard her head spun, and she forgot her own name.

"Thank you," he said softly, with the brightest smile on his face. "I know we are young, but I know that I'm happy about this, and I'm willing to make this work if you let me…"

He trailed off, looking unsure.

"Of course, I'll let you," Evelyn told him.

Then Cameron convinced her to sneak out of school.

She did as he bid, feeling very adventurous as she faked a stomach ache and got the nurse to give her an official pass slip that would allow her to leave early. She figured that since she was pregnant, having cravings, morning sickness, and was extremely tense, she deserved a day out of school.

She felt slightly guilty, but when she saw Cameron waiting at the school gate with his matte black Corvette, the windows rolled down, the guilt fled and was replaced by anticipation and giddiness. First, he took her to the nearest mall and bought clothes and new dresses for her. Then they got some food to satisfy Evelyn's cravings, and lastly, Cameron took her to a jewelry shop, claiming he needed to have his watch fixed.

Once there, Evelyn could not stop looking around. All the diamonds were huge, and the designs were delicate but exquisite, finely suited as if to Evelyn's taste. Finally, her eyes settled on one of the rings by the counter. It was a plain white gold band, inlaid with three princess cut diamonds.

The diamond in the center was larger than the other two, and it had a slightly pink tinge. She had heard about the heart diamond and how rare it was and never expected to see one in real life. Cameron came and stood beside her, following her line of sight.

"Anything that particularly catches your eye?" he asked her quietly.

Evelyn tore her eyes away from the ring and shook her head, smiling up at Cameron brightly.

"Well, I like everything here," she said jokingly. "So…the entire shop?"

Cameron laughed, and suddenly, his eyes were bright. He felt around in his pockets and furrowed his brow.

"Evelyn, I think I forgot my phone at the food court. Can you please go and get it so I can finish up here?"

"Sure!" she agreed and walked off toward where they had been sitting. But she didn't find the phone. She returned to the jewelry store only to see Cameron hurriedly pocketing something and not meeting her eyes.

THE NEIGHBORHOOD

"I couldn't find the phone," she told him, narrowing her eyes suspiciously.

Cameron winced.

"Oh yeah, I'm sorry, baby girl, but I found it on the jewelry counter almost as soon as you left, and I thought I'd just wait for you to come back. You wanna go get some ice cream now?" he asked.

"Yeah, sure!" Evelyn said, smiling contentedly, her suspicion forgotten.

She figured it was just her hormones that were going crazy. What she did not notice, as she turned to walk away in Cameron's embrace, was that the ring she had been staring at was no longer on display.

Chapter 17

The Festival

Evelyn loved Maine.

She loved the lights, the colors, and the people. Even the very air of Maine seemed different somehow, fresher, as if someone had dowsed it with the slightest rose-scented perfume. Michael's brow wrinkled as he tried to find the perfect parking space for the car.

It was his absolute beloved, and somedays Evelyn liked to tease him about how he loved the car more than he loved her. It was a red mustang, the two-seater version, with automatic doors.

"Hurry up, Mike! We're going to be late!" Evelyn prompted. Her face held a giddy smile that made her look decades younger.

"I know. I know," Michael said. "I'm trying, but you know how important it is to park the car right. We need to park it next to the fancier ones."

Evelyn nodded in agreement.

Owners with fancier cars were less likely to be careless with theirs, so there was a lesser chance that they would accidentally chip off the Mustang's paint. It had happened before. Michael found the perfect parking space between a sleek Audi and a silver Mustang.

"Perfect," he whispered with a satisfied smile as he parked the car. They stepped out and were met by a gust of cold wind. Evelyn ran her hands up and down her arm.

Michael silently laid his jacket over Evelyn's shoulder. It was one of those dark ones that went well with her all-black outfit. The only thing that stood out was the way Evelyn's green eyes glittered.

Her smile was bright, and it made Michael feel warm. He had missed seeing her smile. She had started to grow quieter ever since her family had left after the Christmas season, and Michael figured she was slightly bored staying at home alone. At the same time, she waited for the next restaurant branch establishment to be completed.

Her heels knocked against the floor as they started walking.

"Do you have your backup shoes in case you get tired?" Michael asked Evelyn.

Evelyn grinned up at him.

"You know your wife always has a backup plan. So I brought along those red Doc Martin boots you got me last month.

They're comfy, fashionable, and will add a pop of color to my outfit," she said and held up the bag with the boots.

"And I assume you're going to hand this bag over to me to carry while you run off to the booths?" Michael teased, grinning down at her knowingly. Evelyn sent him a guilty glance, already starting to hand him the bag. Michael shook his head fondly and took it from her.

Evelyn could not stop looking at everything. She almost forgot about the way the cobblestone streets chafed against her wedge heels and ran from store to store. There were several vendors lined up on the street selling beautiful trinkets and party hats.

Others were selling lobsters, cotton candy, and other delicacies. Evelyn stopped to buy some blue cotton candy. She bought a chic denim hat for Michael. She even bought a bracelet for Bailey, a watch for Christian, and a knitted scarf for Dora. She loved shopping, and with their restaurants, their individual jobs, and their investments, she knew they wouldn't go broke if they bought a few extra things.

It was still early when they came, so the streets were not crowded, but they slowly started to fill up. Evelyn's empathy started to act up. She could feel the lingering tensions, the joy, and the excitement from the people around them.

THE NEIGHBORHOOD

All those bursts of foreign emotions were still extremely overwhelming for her body. They made her want to cry, laugh, smile, and jump for joy simultaneously, but she could not do all of it at the same time, so she felt frustrated.

Her head felt heavy, and her heart felt full. She moved to the corner and stood in front of a tent. She could spy an antique shop across the street, but she didn't want to encounter the crunch of people to go through it.

Michael turned to look at her as if sensing her unease.

"Are you okay?" he asked.

Evelyn winced.

Of course, Michael would recognize what she was feeling. That was what happened when you lived together for around twelve years. She could pick up on Michael's emotions, and he could pick up on hers. She faked a smile, but she was not sure it convinced him.

"I'm fine. I'm fine. I was just-" Evelyn paused to think. "Waiting for you to go buy me something from the antique shop. I want whatever you buy to be a surprise."

"Huh?" Michael asked, slightly confused.

"This is a test for you. Find me a painting I would like, and we can hang it up in the bedroom. How about that?" Evelyn said.

"That's cheesy," Michael said. "Sure, but do you want me to leave you alone here?"

"I'm not alone," Evelyn said. "I'm going to go check out this tent."

She pointed in a random direction behind her and started walking in its direction. She looked out of the corner of her eye to see Michael watching her.

She looked at the tent before she entered it. It was covered in fabrics of soft purples, shades of grey, and midnight blues, making it look mysterious. Around the front of it was a curtain of beads. She didn't turn to look at Michael as she entered it.

"Here we go," she muttered to herself.

Her eyes fell on the solitary round table in the middle of the room. It was shadowed by slightly translucent curtains beneath which sat a young woman dressed in the deepest shade of purple Evelyn had seen.

Her hair was dark, and her skin was as white as snow. She had her eyes closed, but when she opened them, Evelyn saw that her eyes were white. For a second, Evelyn thought she was blind but then figured that the woman was just wearing lenses.

"Sit," the woman said, and Evelyn obeyed. The woman's skin appearance seemed to change before her very eyes. Her skin turned mocha brown, the color of coffee beans, and her hair became platinum blonde. Her eyes remained white.

The woman smiled, and Evelyn caught her breath because she was beautiful in an almost unearthly way. She thought the appearance change was probably a trick of the light.

"What do I look like to you?" the woman asked.

"You had dark hair and fair skin, but now you have dark skin and white hair," Evelyn said. She was slightly skeptical, but her curiosity overpowered her skepticism, and she stayed put.

"Ah. That's rare. Only one other person has seen me that way. You are a clairaudient," the woman said.

"A clairaudient?" Evelyn asked with a slight tilt of her head.

"Do you feel everyone else's emotions very strongly? Do you have vivid dreams about people who have died? Do you have premonitions about the future? Do you think certain songs come on at specific times, and they seem to be speaking to you?" The woman chanted.

Her voice got louder with every word. Her eyes shifted from blue to black, then to green before settling back on white. Evelyn was scared, terrified actually, but she felt as if she was glued to the spot.

"I do," Evelyn said in a whisper. "I have all of those."

The woman nodded. Her skin settled to a lovely tan, and her hair became a neutral shade of blonde. She looked ordinary now, like everyone else. Even her eyes were blue. It seemed as if her appearance changed according to Evelyn's feelings. When Evelyn felt overwhelmed, the woman seemed to switch her appearance almost constantly, but now that Evelyn was calm, the woman looked almost normal.

"What are you?" Evelyn asked her.

"That's not a question you should ask me. That is a question you should ask yourself. You have gifts that you have been bestowed with just as I have gifts I have been bestowed with," the woman said with a breathtaking smile.

"I don't believe in that. My religion doesn't support," Evelyn told the woman, but her voice was shaky because nothing she had seen just then was normal.

"It does," the woman murmured. Then, she sent Evelyn a determined nod. "The next time you go to church, listen to the hymns about how God grants powers to the ones He wants. God has vessels, and He chooses some amongst us as His vessels."

"I haven't been to Church in a while," Evelyn confessed.

The woman nodded. "I know," she said. "But you must go."

THE NEIGHBORHOOD

"Is there anything you still wish to tell me?" Evelyn asked one final time. Something told her it was time to go, and she was one to always listen to her intuition.

"You have some very powerful spirits looking after you," the woman told Evelyn. "Yes, your grandparents are looking at you from above. And the children you lost…"

The woman paused. Her eyes flashed. "The children you think you lost are there with you."

"In spirit?" Evelyn asked, confused.

"You will know everything in due time. However, you must go now, Evelyn Moskovitz. Your husband is waiting outside with the crystal orb ornament," the woman said.

Evelyn stood up, almost as if her body was not under her control, and started to walk out of the shadowed tent. Michael stood outside with one hand behind his back and a grin on his face. He withdrew the hand, and it held a crystal orb ornament.

"I knew you said you wanted a painting but look at this. It was so cool. And I knew you'd like it," Michael gushed, almost missing the look expression that flashed across Evelyn's face.

She stared at the orb and turned pale.

"Are you okay, my love?" Michael asked.

"I'm fine," Evelyn said, but her voice broke. She cleared her throat and tried again. "I'm fine. Just weak. I think I need some good food."

Evelyn smiled at Michael and knew, at once, that he was not convinced, but he let it go.

"Let's get you some lobster then," he said, stretching one arm around her shoulder as if to catch her in case she fainted.

On the way there, they saw Dora chasing after Bailey and Christian.

"Oh hey, you guys," Dora called out to the couple. "It's nice seeing you here."

Evelyn smiled at Dora, regaining some of her strength. Michael bought her a warm scarf and some cotton candy for a dose of sugar.

"Hi Dora," she said. "Taking the kids out for some festival fun?"

"Yup. They're running off everywhere, and it's hard keeping track of them," Dora sighed tiredly.

For a moment, all Evelyn could see were the wrinkles that lined Dora's eyes and the sad, downward tilt of her mouth. She looked old, frail, and tired all at once. It was as if she was tired of living and taking care of everything. She adored the kids, that was clear, but it was still tough on her to be responsible for everything.

Evelyn felt her expression soften and asked, "How about we take the kids, and you can go and rest. We live next to each other anyway, so it wouldn't be a hassle."

Dora coughed. A loud, raucous cough shook her entire body and left her gasping for breath. Michael extended an arm to steady her, but she declined it. Instead, she stood back up and offered a weak smile to Evelyn.

"Thank you, dear, but are you sure?" she asked.

"Of course, Dora," Michael interjected warmly on Evelyn's behalf. "You go and rest, and I'll send some soup over for that cold."

Dora nodded and smiled at both of them with extreme gratitude. She called Bailey and Christian to explain the situation and then started toward the festival exit.

Bailey and Christian looked at each other, then at Evelyn, and smiled.

"Well, this is going to be fun," Evelyn said, smiling ever so slightly.

Chapter 18

The Big Secret

Bailey and Christian sat in their treehouse. Bailey was pacing this time, and Christian was immersed in a game.

"Bailey Bugs," Christian said with a slightly frustrated sigh. "Can you please sit down? At this rate, you'll stomp a hole through the wooden floor."

Bailey scowled at him, looking so much like Evelyn that it made Christian grin.

"Don't call me that," she snapped. "Only mom is allowed to call me that."

Nonetheless, she sat down beside Christian and picked up a mandala coloring book. Bailey was more into sketching, painting, and reading, whereas Christian was more into sports and comic books.

"Why are you so agitated anyway?" he asked.

"Look, Christian, you already almost blew our bubble during the pool incident, and then there was last night, with the pizza incident. We can not have any more slip-ups. Have you not noticed how mom suspects something already?"

Christian looked away. The pizza incident was his fault and a very careless one at that.

***

Flashback

"You guys want to get some warm pizza?" Michael asked. He had a Santa hat on his head, despite it being nowhere near December, and Evelyn was wearing some reindeer horns that made her look adorable. The cheerful music had put all of them in an extremely good mood, and nobody wanted to go home despite it being almost ten in the night.

"Yes!" Evelyn had cheered, her cheeks slightly flushed with mirth.

Michael laughed and said, "Eight slices of New York Pizza coming right up."

He walked over to the stalls while Evelyn got all of them a warm place at a bench with a colorful umbrella on top of it. Then, in what seemed like no time, Michael put steaming slices of warm pizza in front of them, and they started to dig in.

Christian looked up at Bailey, but she was too busy eating. Human food tasted entirely bland for angels. It had the same taste as water for them. Christian knew that most foods required salt on them, so he took the salt shaker off the table and sprinkled some on his pizza. He met Evelyn's eye across the table as he did so.

Christian took a big bite of his salted pizza.

"Hmm. This is yummy!" he said, giving Evelyn a short thumbs up.

Evelyn had never seen anyone pour salt over pizza before, and she was curious to see what it would taste like. So, she picked up the same salt shaker Christian had used and sprinkled some on her pizza. She took a bite and then choked as a cacophony of tastes hit her tongue.

"This is sweet!" she exclaimed.

She snatched up the bottle and turned it over till she saw the label saying, 'Sugar' on the underside of the bottle. She looked at Christian's pizza in slight disgust.

"This is not salt. It's sugar!" she said, aghast. "How are you eating that?"

Christian panicked.

He had heard of salt, but he had forgotten about sugar also being one of the common human condiments and how easy it was to confuse the two. He started to panic but tried not to let it show on his face. He did not know what to say or do.

THE NEIGHBORHOOD

He tried to explain himself but was cut off by Bailey laughing loudly and obnoxiously beside him. She sent him a glare and continued with her fake laugh.

"Yeah, I'm sorry I did not tell you. My brother is weird. He likes sugar on everything!" Bailey told Evelyn. She was lying, but nobody except Christian knew her well enough to tell.

"On everything?" Michael asked, slightly concerned.

Bailey nodded.

"Oh yes, you should have seen him that one time when he sprinkled sugar over the steak meat that Dora painstakingly made for us. The sight nearly made her faint because of how horrified she was," Bailey continued to lie smoothly.

"Sugar over steak?" Evelyn echoed in disbelief, scrunching her nose.

"Yup," Christian said, jumping in to save the conversation and direct it away from the main topic. "Anyway, that bothered Dora, and she packs my lunches now. You want to know about my school?"

Bailey shook her head at him in panic, fully aware that they could not talk about school or their education either.

"No, let's talk about this book I'm reading!" she said brightly, with a pointed glare at Christian, who balked and immediately nodded and agreed.

It had seemed like a good save, but Evelyn was still slightly suspicious.

***

"Yeah, you're right," Christian said. "No more pizza incidents…or pool ones," he quickly added as an afterthought.

"I think we need to talk to our professors to speed up our human education courses," Bailey said, thoughtfully, tracing circles into the soft blue rug.

"Why, though?" Christian asked, finally shutting off his phone and looking at Bailey. He made a crisscross grid on a piece of paper, found two pencils, and both of them started playing tic tac toe.

"We need to speed up our learning to convince them we're human. Duh," Bailey said, rolling her eyes.

"Right, yeah," Christian agreed. "So what should we learn first?"

"Cooking, human food, and nutrition?" Bailey wondered. "Because those are what we lack in. On the other hand, we picked up human speech, movement, and facial recognition already, and I think we are good at copying human reflexes, too. So, maybe just that for now?"

Christian nodded in agreement and uttered a quick okay. He lost the tic-tac-toe game they were playing and huffed in frustration, picking up his phone again.

"Oh, yeah," he asked, all of a sudden. "Did you remember to give that tear sunflower to mom?"

"Yeah," Bailey said, with a soft smile, as if the memory brought her extreme joy. "She really liked it and put it in the water right away. I did not tell her that it will never wither, for obvious reasons, but I don't think she will notice."

Christian laughed.

"Our mom isn't very perceptive, is she?" he asked.

"Yes," Bailey agreed. "But it's adorable. She's slightly all over the place, and it's so endearing to see her cute smiles every time she sneakily sips some alcohol from her hidden vodka stash."

"You noticed her drinking, too? I think she may be addicted," Christian said, his tone concerned.

"She's not addicted," Bailey said, shaking her head and sending all her hair flying around her face. "She just never managed to recover after she lost us the first time, during her miscarriage."

"Yeah," Christian said. He loved Evelyn, but he knew that Bailey probably understood their mother more than he did since

Bailey was more emotionally intuitive, like their mother.

"So, after that course, we are going to start going to human schools to learn to blend in?" Christian asked Bailey, shifting the topic. He had his eyes fixed on his phone and his tongue between his teeth, trying to concentrate on the game.

"Ah, man. I wish we could just tell mom we aren't human and be done with it. Who cares what our elder says? It's really hard trying to fit in with all the humans," Christian said after a moment of silence between them.

"I know, but the Elder has a certain timeline planned for our mom and dad to get used to us first. We can't just go ahead and botch it up. There are very high chances that our parents would freak out if we do that," Bailey suggested. She was always the voice of reason trying to stop Christian from doing impulsive things.

Christian nodded and went back to his game. Bailey started coloring in her mandala booklet again.

"I'm bored," she complained after a while had passed.

"You want to call Mags over?" Christian asked Bailey.

Her eyes lit up, and she nodded her head enthusiastically.

"Yes, please," she said.

THE NEIGHBORHOOD

She loved Margaret, despite not liking her father, Dale. Since Michael and Dale had been college buddies, Margaret had been placed at Dale's doorstep. The Elder had altered Dale's memories to make him think that Margaret was his daughter and Dale was not the most intelligent of humans, so it had been easier to put him under the Angel Command. Margaret was the one who had lived as a human the longest, and thus, she knew how to blend in with them better than either Christian or Bailey did.

Christian's mind linked with Margaret. That was one of the perks of being non-human. Angels could communicate with one another through mind links. However, Christian and Bailey's mind and the emotional link was stronger because they were twins.

"Mags, you want to come to hang out with us at the treehouse?" Christian asked.

Margaret replied almost immediately, "Ugh, I wish I could. But I'm stuck at this boring date with this human who just won't stop talking about all the places he has been to and all the pretty girls he met in Paris."

Christian laughed aloud, and Bailey looked at him questioningly.

"Are you sure he invited you over for a date? I think all he wanted to do was brag about all his Parisian conquests!" he joked.

He heard Margaret scoff in his head and grinned, glad to know she was not the kind who went for looks over intelligence.

"Oh shit!" Margaret suddenly swore, and Christian lost all the mirth from his face. Bailey noticed his change in expression and wondered what was going on. She linked with Margaret and became part of the now three-way link.

"Are you okay?" Bailey asked Margaret.

"Nope. This bitch just slashed me with a knife, and he's trying to snatch my purse!" Margaret linked back. Her voice sounded frail, and it seemed she was struggling against someone.

"Use your powers to blind him with your light!" Christian said, panicking on Margaret's behalf.

"Nah. That's too dangerous. I wouldn't want anyone to suspect I'm not human," Margaret responded. "I'm right outside the treehouse now. I shouldn't have let him in. That was poor judgment on my part."

Christian exchanged one glance with Bailey and dashed down the stairs to look for Margaret to see if he could help her, but she had already taken care of the situation before he got there. Bailey followed behind Christian, close on his heels.

Margaret stood tall over the body of a slumped man. She was glaring down at him, her cherry red lips twisted into a scowl.

She had bright purple hair that perfectly complimented her tanned skin. Purple was her natural hair coloring, but most humans thought she had dyed it. She was shorter than most women, but something intimidating about her made her look taller than she actually was.

She had a commanding aura, sharp cheekbones, and a tongue that was practically laced with sarcasm. She was older than both Christian and Bailey but only by a couple of years.

"Are you okay?" Bailey asked, looking at Margaret.

"I'm fine," Margaret said, waving off the concern. "I'm just wondering what I need to do with this human here. He tried to attack me."

Christian rolled his eyes.

"He clearly messed with the wrong person. How did he manage to slash you?" he asked.

Margaret held up one hand that had a cut across the wrist, but it was already starting to heal.

"Caught me off guard," Margaret explained shortly. "I'm not particularly proud of it. I guess I should have been more alert."

"Are you going to get that checked out?" Bailey asked, her eyes fixed on the scar.

"It will probably heal on its own anyway," Christian told Bailey, and Margaret nodded.

"Yeah," Margaret said. She alerted the Elder, and all three of them watched as Ruger, another angel disguised as a guard, escorted the man that Margaret had knocked unconscious out of the society. Then all three of them were left alone.

Margaret put one arm over each of their shoulders.

"Now," she said, her voice lowered conspiratorially. "Tell me everything that has been going on around here. You're not allowed to leave even one detail out."

Bailey and Christian exchanged glances with each other as she steered them in the direction of the treehouse.

Chapter 19

Vulnerability

Evelyn shivered and wrapped her arms around herself.

"It's really cold out here," she said to the other girls.

"Yeah. Good thing we got our leggings to wear under the skirts. I'm going to really get a chill if this weather keeps on," one of the girls called back.

It was Friday, and the cheerleading team had assembled beneath the bleachers, convening before the game, huddled on a bench and waiting for it to start. A girl sneezed and then groaned, letting her head fall into her hands.

"How much longer will we have to wait for them?" she asked.

Just as she said that, their school's team started walking into the field.

"About time," Evelyn said, and Kathleen, another cheerleader, rolled her eyes. The cheerleaders still did not like Evelyn.

Amanda, one of the only cheerleaders who liked Evelyn,

turned to her and said, "Anyway. I'm starving. I hope the match ends fast."

Evelyn smiled, "Yeah. I am, too."

Amanda wrinkled her forehead, "You've been starving a lot lately, Eve. You keep complaining about hunger pangs. Do you feel fine?"

Evelyn stiffened and then casually said, "Yeah. My mother has me on this new diet, and I am not used to the constant hunger."

"Oh my God. Eve, you're seventeen. You don't need to diet right now. You're already so skinny!" Amanda exclaimed.

"Yeah, you're right," Evelyn said back, getting into position and starting to cheer when the match began.

It was fifteen minutes into the game when one of the players got injured, so they paused the game to check on the damage. Evelyn glanced at Colson, who was jogging across the field.

"Are you staring at him?" Amanda giggled. "Aww. Your relationship is so cute."

"Actually," Evelyn corrected bashfully. "We aren't really dating anymore. I'm dating Cameron, his twin."

Amanda gasped loudly, eyes wide with delight, and said,

"So you've slept with both of them? You hussy!"

Evelyn quickly shushed her, looking around to make sure nobody had heard.

"No. No, I haven't," she lied through her teeth. She did not want to tell anyone about how she had slept with both brothers.

"But you've kissed them both," Amanda said. It was a statement, not a question, and so Evelyn was not really in a position to deny it. Even if she did deny it, she knew Amanda would not believe her anyway.

"Well…" Evelyn said, trailing off and looking embarrassed.

"So, who's the better kisser?" Amanda asked.

Evelyn gasped, completely mortified. She covered her face with her hands.

"You can't ask me that!" she exclaimed, her ears burning red at the tips.

"Okay, okay," Amanda laughed. "Who is a better boyfriend then?"

Evelyn smiled softly and said, "Cam is. Well, it is not that Colson is bad. It is just that Cameron is more attentive. He knows what I want, and he can read my moods. Kisses from him feel like fireworks. It was never like that with Colson. With Cam, there is just a lot of-"

"Chemistry?" Amanda finished for her. She had a smug grin on her face.

"You're seriously in love with him," she told Evelyn decisively.

"Yeah, I am," Evelyn said, a soft smile playing around the corners of her lips.

Just then, she caught movement out of the corner of her eye. She turned to see Cameron moving toward the cheerleader benches with his eyes fixed on her.

"Oh my god. He's staring at me!" Kathy, one of the meaner cheerleaders, squealed excitedly. Evelyn did not turn to look at her.

The girls' squealing got louder as he got closer.

"Why are you here?" Evelyn asked him when he stopped right in front of her. The other cheerleaders started to scowl, their excitement turning to disgust.

"Why is he talking to her?" One of them asked another, and Cameron overheard.

"I'm talking to her because she is my girlfriend, and I came here today just to see her," Cameron said, turning to the blonde girl and glaring at her. Evelyn heard whispers startup around them and winced.

"Are you here to see the match?" she asked him softly.

He smirked and said, "Nope. I'm here to see you."

"Cameron!" Evelyn whined, hiding her face in his chest. "They're only going to spread more rumors about me now."

Cameron lifted her up, spun her around, kissed her, and then let her back onto her feet.

"Let them talk. They need to know you're my only priority, and if anyone messes with you, they're going to have to deal with me."

Evelyn rolled her eyes playfully.

"What are you? A caveman?" she asked with a scoff.

"When it comes to you? Yes," Cameron told her. "I'm waiting for you outside. Once you are done with the match, find my car. I have a surprise for you."

He kissed Evelyn one last time and, before she could stop him, started walking toward the direction of the parking lot.

When the match ended, Evelyn found him sitting in his car, the heater on full blast in an attempt to stave off the winter chill. Evelyn sat beside him, offering him some popcorn she had brought with her.

Cameron ignored the popcorn and slid his hand up her thighs, scowling when his hands met the fabric of her sparkly leggings.

"What's this?" he scoffed.

"That is Cam proofing," Evelyn said with a grin, proud of herself.

"I can rip that clean off with my teeth, babe," Cameron told her slowly.

Evelyn blushed and shifted away from the hand on her thigh. Cameron drew his hand back, reaching around to try and ruffle Evelyn's hair instead. Evelyn smacked his hand away and pouted.

"Where is that surprise you promised you would have for me? Evelyn asked.

"All in due time, sweetheart," Cameron said, turning the ignition and beginning to drive.

"I got you some clothes. Your mother packed them for me," Cameron said as he drove. "We are not going home tonight."

"My mother?" Evelyn asked, aghast and slightly mortified. "You told her you're going to take me out and to give you a change of clothes for me? Oh God, Cam! She probably thinks we are sleeping together!"

"Well, we are," Cameron smirked at Evelyn.

Evelyn opened the bag and sifted through the clothing inside. It comprised mostly of lingerie and short dresses.

"Cam!" Evelyn screeched. "You asked my mother to pack me lingerie?"

Cameron started laughing and said, "I knew you would freak out. But no, I asked Saleen. Of course, I did not know she would pack all that, but I guess she knows us pretty well by now."

"Where are we going, anyway?" Evelyn asked Cameron.

"Nah, uh. Not telling you. You'll see when we get there," Cameron said.

"Are you kidnapping me?" Evelyn asked teasingly.

"Hmm. Maybe I am," Cameron told her.

Evelyn side-eyed him. She thought of how many women had sat in his car and been driven around by him to shopping malls and hotel rooms. She did not want to be just a number on his list or a notch on his bedpost.

She cared so deeply about Cameron that it almost terrified her sometimes. He meant a lot to her, but she was unsure if his feelings were as intense as hers. He had told her, time and time again, that he loved her, that he had eyes only for her, and that she may not have been his first, but she was definitely his last.

He had made her feel loved and cared for, but the scared, insecure part of Evelyn prevented her from believing him. She had been taunted for her looks, dark hair, and green eyes for so long that she had started hating those aspects of her.

She did not think she was pretty or beautiful. She saw no reason why Cameron would like her.

She felt the urge to do something impulsive. Holding the edge of her yellow top, she lifted it off her head. She was wearing bright pink underwear underneath.

Cameron stopped the car, parking it to the side.

"Holy-" he began to say but stopped himself from speaking. Instead, he scanned Evelyn, took a deep breath, closed his eyes, and when he reopened them, his gaze was focused and clear.

Evelyn kicked off her leggings and skirt, trying to prompt him to look at her body.

"Am I not attractive enough for you?" she asked.

Cameron whipped his head around to look at her so fast that she almost heard his neck crick.

"Not beautiful enough for me? Eve, what are you talking about?" he said. His eyes stayed on her face, holding her gaze.

"You're not even looking at me. It's almost like I don't even affect you. You don't need to stay with me out of some sense of obligation because I am pregnant, Cam," Evelyn said, looking away.

Cameron lifted a hand toward her and shifted her face to look at him again.

"What is going on, Eve? Where is all this coming from?" he asked, his voice soft as if he did not want to scare her. However, he realized she felt very vulnerable, and he wanted to be as careful with her as possible.

"I don't know, Cam. Why won't you look at me?" Evelyn asked, her voice near hysterics.

All her doubts came back to the forefront of her mind, and everything Cameron did only seemed to confirm that he was playing her.

Cameron's eyes flared in anger, glaring at Evelyn, but his touch on her face never tightened, still holding her in the gentlest of ways.

"The reason I am not looking at you, Evelyn, is because I know that if I look at you, I won't be able to hold myself back from fucking you so thoroughly you won't be able to walk for days. And I don't mind doing that, but I don't want to hurt our child, the one that I am already so in love with, because I know and love its mom," he said. His voice was not loud, but it was brimming with carefully controlled anger.

A tear fell from Evelyn's eye and rolled down her cheek, falling on Cameron's fingers.

"All those girls that you have been with, the blondes, the models, I can't-" Evelyn began to say.

"You don't need to," Cameron said, cutting her off. "All those models, those girls that came before you, none of them mean anything to me now, Evelyn, because now I have you. All of them were just me trying to fill some sort of gap in my heart, and now that you've come along and filled it, I don't need anything else. Evelyn, don't you understand? You are my completion! You are my beginning and my end. My future. When I'm looking at you, I'm looking at my future."

"You love me?" Evelyn asked in a small voice, another tear falling from her eye.

"I love you," Cameron affirmed, eyes fixed on her. He brushed his thumb across her cheek, catching her tear before it could fall.

He shed his jacket and put it on her shoulders, guiding her arms through it and zipping it up from the front. Then he restarted the car and continued driving till they came to a fancy hotel.

It had high chandeliers, posh furniture, and Persian carpets. Evelyn doubted she would ever be able to step foot into a place as grand as this if it were not for Cameron. She felt small, naked, and inadequate in his jacket, but Cameron lifted her in his arms.

He carried her, as if she was a newly married bride, up the hotel threshold. He kept her head down, asking her to ignore the stares while he stood at the receptionist desk and asked for the keys to the honeymoon suite that he had reserved. He set her down only when they were safely inside the door.

Evelyn took a minute to take in the warm wood flooring and the dim lighting. She could smell flowers, peonies and lilies, and Cameron's perfume. She focused on him as he turned up the heat in the room, making sure Evelyn was not cold. He turned on the music, and a slow waltz started playing throughout the room.

He held her hand out, waiting for Evelyn to feel ready enough to put her hand in his. When she did so, he led her in a silent waltz. They did not speak. They did not need to speak. Cameron understood the emotional turmoil that Evelyn was going through.

He hated himself for being the cause of her pain, and he wished, more than anything, to go back into the past, just so he could prevent his younger self from being a huge playboy.

They stood there, foreheads touching, long after the waltz was over. Evelyn closed her eyes. She felt Cameron shifting in front of her and letting go of her hands. She still kept her eyes closed. She did not want to move on from the moment, the silence and longing that they had just shared.

"Open your eyes," Cameron said in a whisper. Evelyn obeyed.

Cameron was bending in front of her, on one knee, holding a ring in one hand, ready to put it on her finger.

"Evelyn. I can't ask you to marry me because I'm terrified you will say no. So, I am begging you. Evelyn-" his voice broke off midway. "Eve, I love you. Please, please marry me. To promise, I will cherish you for the rest of my life. I promise you will be the last thought in my mind before I die. I promise that, when I die, I will wait for you at heaven's gates, refusing to go in without you. Evelyn, the love of my life, mother of my child. I am begging you, right here, right now, to let me be in your life. Please say yes."

Evelyn felt her heart stop. She felt transfixed by the way Cameron's eyes seemed to glow with fire with passion and honesty. The sincerity in his words and the suddenness of the proposal struck her, but she knew, more than anything, that she wanted to spend her entire life with the man before her.

THE NEIGHBORHOOD

She nodded, and he slid the ring on her finger. It was the same ring she had once been looking at when they went shopping. He had seen it.

Cameron stood up; a smile flitted over his face.

"Words, my love. I need to hear your words," he whispered to her.

"Yes," Evelyn said, beginning to smile, hating the tears that once more filled her eyes.

"Yes," Evelyn said again, louder.

Cameron pulled her closer, grinned, dipped his face close to hers, and pulled her into a breathtaking kiss.

Chapter 20

Planning Trips and Dreams

The room was stuffy; the sun was high in the sky and hotter than usual. The neighborhood was covered by the glass dome, which meant that the sun's ultraviolet rays got filtered out and ensured that none of the residents got a sunburn, but the dome, unfortunately, was not temperature controlled.

"It's so humid," Evelyn complained with a pout. She was making one of her favorite raspberry smoothies with extra bananas. They were healthy, and unlike most healthy smoothies, were not disgusting.

She slipped a straw into her glass and dropped in two ice cubes.

"I know!" Michael groaned. "I had to be out in the head doing the grunt work today. We have a couple of new construction workers, and they had to be guided."

He shook his head in dismay.

"Wish we could take a break. Maybe go somewhere cooler," Evelyn lamented, pushing her frizzy, dark hair away from her face. She had long hair that curled up ever so slightly at the bottom, but they seemed always turned into a horrendous, frizzy mess during the more humid weather.

"How about we go camping?" Michael asked, his eyes lighting up. He set down the TV remote and turned fully to look at Evelyn in the kitchen. Evelyn fixed her eyes on the football game playing on television and wrinkled her nose in distaste.

"Camping?" she asked. "In this heat?"

Michael shook his head and said, "Not now. In a few days, the weather is predicted to be better. I think-" he paused slightly. "We could go camping the day after tomorrow. There is this place outside Boston that is only two hours away from here. I scouted it out when we were doing construction work near that site. We can go there on Friday, spend the weekend there and come back on Monday. What do you think?"

Evelyn nodded her head.

"Yeah, that sounds good," she agreed. She took a sip of her smoothie, letting her eyebrows wrinkle in thought.

"Just us?" she asked.

Michael looked slightly taken aback.

"Yeah, I thought we could have some *"us"* time."

"I kind of don't want to be alone. We've never been to Boston, and we don't know if it will be completely safe. But, there is protection in numbers, so maybe we could get our neighbors to go with us?" Evelyn confessed.

"Yeah, you're right!" Michael said, turning back to the television, just as his favorite team scored a goal. He cheered, and Evelyn rolled her eyes but let a fond smile cross her lips. He looked back at Evelyn during the highlights. He reckoned that he could just watch the recorded version of the game later.

His conversation with his wife was more important to him. Michael was the kind of person who believed in making time for his loved ones. He put in extra effort to spend time with Evelyn, even if it meant missing out on work, his favorite games, and his hobbies.

He knew that Evelyn was the most important part of his life, his most important person, and he liked doing little things for her. It was just that Evelyn always seemed to live inside her head, and he did not know if she ever recognized the little sacrifices that he made for her.

"I wish I could ask our family to come with, but they're mostly out of the state for the time being. I really hope they move in with us," Evelyn said, mindlessly stirring the straw in her smoothie.

Michael stood up from the couch with a sigh. He walked behind Evelyn and wrapped his arms around her waist, turning her to face him.

"What?" Evelyn asked, but he did not reply.

Instead, he leaned his head down to take a sip from the straw she held between her fingers. Evelyn's eyes went wide. Michael flashed her a smile and took the mug from her hands, placing it on the countertop. He backed her into it till she had no other place to look.

He was so close that she could smell his perfume and count every freckle on his otherwise perfect skin. Evelyn usually liked facial hair on men because it made them look older. Still, Michael already looked like a walking Abercrombie model with that sharp jawline, which made him look mature, so she did not think he really needed one.

He placed a hand on her waist and pulled her closer, cupping the back of her neck with his other hand. Then he kissed her, a slow, dizzying kiss that tasted like the sweet smoothie he had just drunk.

Michael licked his bottom lip, smirking in satisfaction at the frazzled expression on Evelyn's face.

"You taste sweet. I want more," he said.

He started walking away from her, done with the conversation. He sat back on the couch and unmuted the television. Evelyn scowled.

"Oh, hell no," she said, striding up to him and sitting on his lap. "You can't just kiss me like that and then go back to watching TV, Mike. You have to finish what you started."

"Finish what I started?" Michael asked her innocently. He blinked his eyes up at her, but the glimmer of mischief within their blue depths gave away that this was what he expected.

Evelyn kissed him, pulling him by the collar and allowing her tongue to explore his mouth. She pulled back and grinned down at his dazed expression.

"You taste sweet," she said, mimicking what he had done earlier.

Michael scowled and pulled her closer, kissing her neck and down her collar bone. His lips curled into a smirk when he heard Evelyn gasp. He loved the effect he had on her. He undid the lacing holding her shirt together and slid the strap of her bra down her shoulder before unhooking it and pulling it off completely.

Evelyn fumbled, unbuttoning the front of his shirt. She ran a manicured nail down his chest, and he groaned, capturing her wandering hands and pinning them to the couch. Evelyn moaned when he rubbed a rough thumb over one of her nipples. She arched her back, allowing him to do whatever he wanted with her.

He left wet, openmouthed kisses down the middle of her chest, stopping at her belly button and nipping at it playfully. Evelyn gasped, her body jerking in response. He had never done that before, in fact, nobody had ever done that before, and she liked it.

Michael turned them so that Evelyn was lying on the couch. He folded his hands around her hips, keeping them down because she had started bucking, and it was only making it harder for him to not fuck her raw.

"You like that?" he asked, his voice gravelly and dripping with lust.

Evelyn nodded, watching him worship her body through half-closed eyes. Michael unbuttoned her jeans and pulled them down her legs, along with her panties. He pushed his weight onto his arms, pausing just to look at her. He slipped one finger along her opening, nudging her open but not entering her. Then he moved his fingers. His fingers felt rough against her soft flesh.

"Mike!" Evelyn called out, intending it to sound like a warning, but it came out as a moan.

"Stop playing with me," she wanted to tell him, but the

words would not come out of her mouth.

Michael smirked at her, knowing exactly what he was doing to her. He looked at her once, his eyes intense, daring her to stop him and knowing he had complete control of her pleasure. He dipped his head and licked once before allowing his tongue to enter her. Evelyn screamed.

Her legs automatically wrapped around his head, and her hands went to his hair, pulling him closer. Michael lapped at her core, trying not to choke. He eased her hands from around his head before pulling his tongue out of her and sucking. That was what tipped Evelyn over the edge, and she orgasmed, gasping through it.

She could swear she blanked out, almost seeing stars. After a few seconds, when she came to, she saw Michael grinning at her wolfishly. His face held mirth, but his eyes were filled with warmth. Michael was the only man who pleasured her without expecting her to do the same for him.

He was the only man who had gone down on her, and he was the only man who had learned, over time, how to satisfy her completely. Making love with him was intense, but it was also gratifying. It allowed them to feel closer to each other afterward.

He tucked her in, covering her with a sheet. Then he looked down at himself and blushed.

THE NEIGHBORHOOD

"Yeah, I'm going to go take a cold shower," he told her. Evelyn almost laughed. It was hilarious the way he had just made love to her, did things with her body that nobody else had done before, and felt shy afterward. She drifted off into a light sleep.

***

"Evelyn?"

Evelyn heard someone call her. She opened her eyes and looked around. She was standing in a field that was filled with sunflowers, millions and millions of sunflowers, as far as the eye could see. She turned and saw a stream of pure, glistening water. It seemed almost transparent because of how clear it was.

"Evelyn!"

The voice called again, this time excitedly. Evelyn looked around, and her eyes caught an angel sitting by the rocks around the water. She had long, flowing white hair that reached her mid-back and was dressed in a white sundress. Her skin glowed with a healthy tan.

She turned her head, and Evelyn felt her breath catch in her throat. She was beautiful.

"Come," the angel said, prompting her closer. Evelyn went closer till she was standing in front of her. Only then she noticed the angel was holding a bundle of cloth. She looked closer till she

realized that it was not a bundle of cloth, it was a child!

The angel nodded at Evelyn, gesturing for her to take the child. Evelyn did as she bid, gasping in awe as soon as the baby was in her arms. It was a girl with dark hair. Her eyes were closed, so Evelyn could not see their color.

Evelyn felt as if her heart was expanding, almost as if it would burst. Tears rolled down her cheek, but she did not know why she was crying. The child was so beautiful that Evelyn could not stop looking away from her. She gently pushed a strand of hair away from the baby's forehead, running a finger over the baby's nose. She poked the small, open palm, and it curled around her finger.

A sob escaped Evelyn's mouth.

"Oh god!" she muttered. She felt as if her soul had been stabbed thousand times over, wrenched from her body. She felt extreme heartbreak but, at the same time, extreme euphoria, as if she knew that as long as the child was in her arms, she would be willing to go through hell and back.

The baby fidgeted in her arms but did not lose her grip over Evelyn's fingers.

She opened her eyes, and Evelyn gasped.

Green eyes, exactly like hers.

THE NEIGHBORHOOD

***

Evelyn woke up with a gasp, her body bolting into a sitting position. She did not understand what had just happened. All she knew was that she had seen an angel and a baby. She felt, in her heart, that the baby was hers. She just knew.

She looked around to see that it was dark. She still had to make calls to everyone about the camping plans. She checked in with them, one by one, but suspiciously enough, none of them seemed to be available for the weekend. That was until she called Miss Dora.

"Hey Dora?" she said, locking eyes with Michael, who had just walked into the room. He had a plate of warm food in his hand, and he gestured to it, asking her to eat.

She held up her hand.

"Hey, Evelyn. Thank you for calling, dearie. Is everything okay?" Dora asked.

Dora's sweet voice made Evelyn smile.

"Yes. It is just that Michael and I were planning on going camping, and we wondered if you and the children would like to join us?" Evelyn asked.

She was suddenly nervous, but she did not understand why.

She dismissed it.

"Yes. Of course, let me just confirm it with them," Dora said, and Evelyn immediately felt a smile cross her lips. She could hear the twins cheering wildly in the background and knew, at once, that they had begged Dora to agree.

"The twins are very eager about it," Dora told Evelyn with a slight laugh.

"Yes, I can hear them," Evelyn laughed.

They said their goodbyes, and Evelyn hung up the phone.

'A camping trip in the cabin with just us and the children. I wonder how that will go,' Evelyn mused to herself.

Epilogue

The ride to the camping cabin was silent.

They had not brought the dogs along with them, as per Michael's suggestion, because he suggested that it would allow them to spend more quality time with the children. Michael and Evelyn were sitting in the front, in terse silence, preparing for what they were about to tell the kids.

Christian and Bailey were sitting in the backseat. They had been told about their "father's" death just a week ago. He may not have been their actual father, but he still had been the angel guardian they had been assigned, and it felt like a huge loss to them. However, they did not know how long they could pretend to be in their same earthly forms, and they had both decided to tell Evelyn the truth.

Evelyn and Michael, however, were both already planning on adopting the children. They had been thinking about it ever since Dora had told them that the children's father had died.

"Are you guys alright?" Michael turned back to ask once they had finally stopped at the cabin. "I know Dora told you about-"

Evelyn elbowed Michael in the ribs to get him to stop speaking. He coughed and scowled, holding his side.

"Yeah," Bailey said, giving Michael a sad smile. "We will be okay. Thank you for taking us on this trip for a change of scenery."

Evelyn smiled and held the door open for the family to walk in. They trudged over the warm, wooden floors, taking in the cozy interior and huge windows. They all sat around the fireplace while Evelyn poured all of them warm cocoa from the thermos that she had prepared.

She longed for some alcohol, and she knew she would need some to get through the trip, but she was also aware that she needed to keep her head.

She handed a cup to Michael, then to Bailey, and then Christian.

"Thank you, mom," Christian said when she handed him his hot chocolate. Bailey looked at Christian and smiled. The elders had not planned for this, but the twins knew this was what they needed to do. They had decided that they would tell Evelyn everything during the cabin trip.

Michael fell silent, unsure about how he should let this play out. He could understand how Evelyn was feeling, and he knew that she wanted to let the children explain. She had gone completely still and was staring at Christian's face.

"What did you say?" Evelyn asked, her voice shaking.

"He said thank you," Bailey said, explaining for Evelyn.

"He called me mother," Evelyn said. Her voice broke, and her eyes started to tear up. "Is this some sort of sick joke? You-"

Evelyn looked at Bailey, and everything seemed to stop. Bailey's eyes were bright and clear, green, like the child she had seen in her dreams. She looked at Christian, and he, too, seemed familiar. She had a slight feeling that they were her children.

They were the children she had lost, along with Cameron, in that car accident sixteen years ago. That was when she had realized what her dreams had been trying to tell her all along.

"I know," she told them. "You're Christian and Bailey. *My* Christian and Bailey, aren't you?"

Michael looked confused, but he did not say anything. Finally, Bailey nodded, and that was all it took for Evelyn to pull her into a hug.

"How? I don't understand. How is any of this possible?" Evelyn asked, her tears falling down her cheeks.

Christian joined the group hug, and Evelyn was suddenly

filled with a sense of completeness. She realized it was the first time she had ever felt complete since she lost her unborn babies. She did not want to understand. It was enough that they were there with her, somehow.

When you lose someone in life, and they come back to you, it does not matter how they got there. What matters more is that they are finally there. So Evelyn felt that nothing mattered except the children.

She could still remember the day she lost them.

**

Evelyn giggled as she and Cameron drove through the slight drizzle. They had been on a picnic date and were hurrying home because it had started raining. Cameron was serenading her with cheesy love songs and trying to make her smile. He had his eyes fixed on the road, and he wanted to make sure they got home soon because he did not want Evelyn to catch a cold.

"Knock knock?" Cameron asked.

"Who's there?" Evelyn giggled. He had recently been very into knock-knock jokes, and Evelyn was always happy to humor him. She knew most people would scoff at his jokes, but they made her laugh, and that was the only thing that mattered.

"Tank," Cameron said.

"Tank who?" Evelyn asked, laughing as they neared the punchline.

"Th-"

Cameron began to say, but a car appeared out of nowhere. Cameron swerved to avoid hitting it, and his car slid for a second before it began to roll over. It rolled once, then twice, then a third time. That was when Evelyn hit her head against the window and blanked out.

When she regained consciousness, she was in a hospital bed. She was told that she had lost her children, her precious twins, and her fiancé and that she was lucky to be alive. But Evelyn did not feel lucky.

She felt like she wanted to die. She had finally found a place she belonged and a person who loved her. She had always wanted to be a mother, and she was getting her to wish of being one, but fate snatched it all away from her.

At Cameron's funeral, all she could think about was the one knock-knock joke that he had never finished. He had never been able to finish his last words. Her babies had never gotten to take their first steps, and she had never gotten a family photo of all four of them together.

There were so many hopes, so many dreams, and all of

them had been left incomplete. Evelyn never told anyone about the last moments with Cameron in the car. That last moment and that the last joke was a personal moment that would always remain between her, Cameron, and the unborn children in her womb. It hurt too much to speak of them because she felt that if she did, the moment would lose its importance. She was afraid to let it go.

***

Bailey broke out from the hug and wiped the tears that had escaped her eyes.

Christian moved away a second later. Evelyn wanted to protest. She wanted them back in her arms, but she knew she had to get a grip of her emotions.

"Mother?" Christian asked.

Evelyn turned to look at him. Her heart melted when he called her mother. She wanted to scream and shout, dance in absolute glee. She wanted to climb up to the Empire State building and announce that she was a mother and her kids were with her.

"Knock knock?" Christian asked. A tear escaped his eye. Evelyn reached out and wiped it away.

"Who's there?" she asked.

Her heart stuttered. He looked so much like Cameron at that moment - she did not understand how she had never seen it before. But she saw it now. She realized then that she knew all along that they were her kids. That was why she had grown as attached to them as fast as she had.

She had known, but part of her had been too terrified to give her false hope, so she had denied it, again and again, till she completely blocked out those thoughts from her head.

She recalled the way she had jumped into the pool for Christian and the way she had bought an expensive butterfly hairpin for Bailey back when she had known them for barely a week. She had always known that she loved them, but she did not know why.

"Tank," Christian said, and Evelyn dropped the cup she was holding.

Luckily, it was empty, and the floor had a rug on it, so it did not break. Michael looked back and forth between Evelyn and the children. He did not understand what was happening, but he knew he had to allow them their private moment. So he busied himself with picking the cup Evelyn had just dropped, briefly kissed Evelyn's forehead, and left the room.

"Tank who?" Evelyn asked.

"Tank you!" Christian said, then again, slower, "Thank. You."

Evelyn laughed, even as tears poured from her eyes. It was not even funny. She wished she could go back in time and roll her eyes at how lame the joke was. She wished that she could have heard it from Cameron's mouth. She wished Cameron, too, was alive.

"Thank you for existing, mom. Thank you for moving on. Thank you for not giving up and staying strong. You have done so well. We've been watching over you, and dad has been watching over you. He wants you to know that he is proud of you for making it through. He wants you to be happy. All dying people get one last wish, and he used his wish to grant you eternal happiness. But he knew you would be too depressed if you lost us. So, after he died, he pleaded with the angel court for us to be sent back as angels to look after you. The court chose you as a suitable candidate for not one but two guardians," Bailey said warmly, smiling at Evelyn.

"Dad told us to tell you that he loves you and that he will forever love you," Christian added.

Evelyn started to sob. She was bawling like a child, her head between her shoulders, and her kids watched her. They knew that she was crying happy tears. They waited till she was done. Her eyes were red, and she was sniffling, but her face held a teary smile.

She pulled the twins into a hug again, and they stayed like

that for a long while till Bailey said, "I have something to give you, mom."

Evelyn was still not used to being called "mom." Her heart ached with a sweet sort of pain every time one of the twins called her that.

"What is it?" Evelyn asked and watched patiently as Bailey shuffled around in her bag, looking for something.

Finally, she pulled out a single solitary sunflower, and Evelyn stared at it in marvel. It was the most beautiful sunflower she had ever seen. None of the petals were broken or bruised, and they were all curled slightly inward, almost as if they had been molded.

It was so beautiful it almost looked unreal, and Evelyn expected it to be a glass sculpture. But then Bailey handed it to Evelyn, and she could feel its petals under her fingers, the texture letting her know that it was very much a real sunflower.

"It's called an angel sunflower. It grows from the tears of an angel, and it never withers. It is eternal, like an angel's love. The only thing that kills it is if a cruel person holds it. When someone with a blackened heart holds the sunflower, it withers, and when someone with a pure heart holds it, it glows. Look, it's glowing right now!" Bailey pointed out, and it was true. The sunflower was glowing between Evelyn's fingers.

There was a knock on the door, and everyone looked up to see Michael standing at the entrance of the door.

"So… is anyone going to fill me in on the exciting details or nah?" he asked offhandedly, in that joking way of his, immediately lightening the mood.

He came and sat down as the kids began explaining everything from the beginning. As they did so, Evelyn looked around at all of them, at her little family, and her heart swelled.

"I love them!" she whispered to herself. She knew she loved them. Of course, she did, but saying it out loud seemed to make it more permanent. She sat there, watching the twins animatedly explain everything to her soulmate, and she realized that she finally felt complete.

Made in the USA
Columbia, SC
17 October 2022